To J.

" This Laughs On Me "

Emilio Paletta

NEVER SAY UNCLE

by

EMILIO PALETTA

authorHOUSE

1663 LIBERTY DRIVE, SUITE 200
BLOOMINGTON, INDIANA 47403
(800) 839-8640
www.authorhouse.com

This book is a work of fiction. Places, events, and situations in this story are purely fictional. Any resemblance to actual persons, living or dead, is coincidental.

First published by AuthorHouse 04/05/04

ISBN: 1-4184-1828-5 (e)
ISBN: 1-4184-1829-3 (sc)

Printed in the United States of America
Bloomington, Indiana

This book is printed on acid free paper.

Edited by Emilio Paletta
Designed by Emilio Paletta

Dedication

Special thanks to the following:

God almighty for the blessed gifts he has bestowed upon me, My beloved wife of 51 glorious years for her devotion, understanding, and encouragement.

My wonderful children, Joanne and Anthony Jordan, and Robert Paletta.

My precious and talented grandchildren Erica and Mark Jordan.

To *Golden Agers* wherever they may be, and their forefathers.

To all who face adversity, *never say uncle!*

For all the help and patience that Anthony, Joanne, and Erica displayed.

Thanks to Merilda Wilkerson. (Cover Artwork)

Finally to the elderly living in health care facilities throughout the world and to those unsung heroes dedicated to their care and well-being. "God Bless them all."

Table of Contents

Prologue

Once upon a time, today's seniors lived in neighborhoods. They were the product of another generation, born during the Great Depression and World War II. Back then, they never had a care or realized how sweet their young lives were.

Their neighborhoods, for the most part, were ethnically integrated, each different, yet the same. They were a blend of nationalities and multicultures, bound together by a common thread. All God's children, they were all Americans. The neighborhood was their sanctuary, a place where everyone knew and looked out for one another. They had safe havens where front doors were seldom locked and crime was a non-event. Young and old alike, they all had nicknames.

Rain-flooded streets following a thunderstorm became instant swimming pools. When dry, they served as playgrounds for games of stickball, kick-the-can, and red light, to name a few. Everything from the house of worship to the local movie house was within walking distance. Memories of yesteryear remain etched in their minds.

How can they ever forget sitting on the edge of their seats during a Saturday matinee munching on Jujubes, waiting for the "hoopla" to begin? Those hair-raising nail-biting chases, breathtaking battles, and phenomenal escapes, by their heroes and heroines will never fade from memory.

Hundreds of serials, including *Flash Gordon, Spy Smasher, Buck Rogers,* and *Tailspin Tommy,* involved but a handful of their heroes. They sat captivated, watching fearless cowboys the likes of Tom Mix, Hop-a-Long Cassidy, Ken Maynard, and Buck Jones round up the desperados before riding off into the sunset.

When the "jig was up," the detectives Sherlock Holmes, Dick Tracy, Bulldog Drummond, and Charlie Chan "always got their man." I'll bet if the kids of that era close their peepers, they're still able to see those unforgettable words, once flashed across the screen at chapter's end, "To Be Continued…"

December 7, 1941, many of them were seated in their favorite movie houses. On that Sunday around 3 p.m., the theater manager walked onto the stage. As house lights went up and projectors stopped rolling, he made that memorable announcement "All military personnel are ordered to return to their base immediately." At the time, Errol Flynn's "reel fans" sat watching his portrayal of General George Armstrong Custer in the now-classic *They Died with Their Boots On.*

Buzzing could be heard throughout the theater as servicemen rose to leave. Fearing the worst, the rest followed suit. They were anxious to hurry home for an update. Though, I must say, they must have felt a bit guilty leaving Mr. Flynn alone to make his last stand at Little Big Horn.

Once home, they learned that in a sneak attack, the Japanese bombed Pearl Harbor. Wishing to vent their anger, they smashed those junky knickknacks marked "Made in Japan" and threw them into the trashcan.

From that day forward, old neighborhoods changed forever as older siblings, relatives, friends, and neighbors marched off to war. They became the real-life heroes. Young and old, those left behind chipped in, doing their part to defeat the enemy. Under their commander-in-chief, F.D.R., they pledged to destroy the axis powers of Japan and Germany, vowing to *never say uncle.*

There's one thing more; through it all, they never lost their sense of humor.

Introduction

Before turning to Chapter 1, think back to another time and place. Perhaps I can help? The setting is the courtyard during lunch hour. You're one of hundreds of young kids taking a break from schoolwork. While playing tag with friends, the school bully approaches. For no foreseen reason, other than getting a kick out of picking on smaller kids, he goads you into a confrontation.

"Knock the stick off my shoulder," he demands, attempting to embarrass you in front of your classmates. Thinking you're no match for him, you comply, even though it means getting the crap kicked out of you.

During the scuffle, the bully eventually pins you down. Before releasing you from a stranglehold, he demands you "cry uncle." Suddenly your adrenaline begins to flow as you hear the voices of friends shouting, "Never say uncle!" Inspired by their cries, you fight with all your might, turning the tables, freeing yourself from your adversary's hold. In that brief moment, your life changes forever, as *never say uncle* becomes your mantra, preparing you to face any challenge that may come your way.

With that thought in mind, please read on. Follow the journey of fellow human beings who like you, would *never say uncle*. Along the way, grab a few old-fashioned laughs for good luck.

Chapter 1
The First Meeting

"'You're not getting up 'til you cry uncle, you little twerp,' was the ultimatum Lemonhead bellowed after pinning me down. As he began applying pressure, trying to choke the living hell out of me, I felt as if my eyeballs were about to pop from their sockets. Due to the lack of oxygen, my head began pounding, as everything turned topsy-turvy. I was about ready to give in to that bully, when suddenly I heard you egging me on, shouting words of encouragement. Do you remember the incident, Carmen?" asked Sonny.

"Sure I do!" said Carmen. "Like it was yesterday."

"What was it you told me?" asked Sonny.

"Don't do it, Sonny," Carmen said. "You can take him. He's nothing more then a paper tiger!"

"Yes, that's right," said Sonny. "You told me something else I've never forgotten." Carmen thought for a second.

"Now I remember," said Carmen. "I said no matter what, *never say uncle!*"

"Right again" said Sonny. "Furthermore, I was surprised to hear you say I was neglecting family and friends to go on a wild goose chase. That bothered me."

After Sonny's mother passed away, he became despondent, fearing the only link to his heritage was gone. Neglecting all who were near and dear, he set out on what seemed to be a futile search. Determined not to give in, recalling that childhood catch phase, he plodded on. His goal was to find his mother's brother, whom he hadn't seen in over 50 years. Knowing that if he succeeded, he would regain contact with his glorious heritage.

During their discussion, Carmen asked, "What if your uncle is dead? You realize you're playing a long shot."

"So be it" said Sonny, "I must have closure. I must know one way or other, before I can resume my once-normal life." He continued, "Let me put it in terms you'll understand. The year is 1944, December 16th, you and the men of the 101st Glider Regiment are fighting for your lives. You're

1

starving, it's freezing cold, and you're bogged down at the Battle of the Bulge. Tell me, Carmen, did you guys quit?"

"Hell no, though at times we felt like it."

"When the Nazi commandant asked General McAuliffe to surrender, what did he tell him?" asked Sonny.

"Nuts," Carmen answered. "'Nuts' is what he told that bastard!"

"Now do you understand what I mean?" asked Sonny. "No matter what challenge comes our way, big or small, we must hang tough and *never say uncle*. It's guys like us who came from the neighborhoods of America, where we learned the hard way, anything worthwhile is worth fighting for. For that reason, I refuse to throw in the towel until I find my uncle." Sonny gave his old buddy a hug, as they went their separate ways.

That evening, as Sonny and his wife Jo sat around the dinner table, the silence was broken by the ringing of the phone. Picking up the receiver, Sonny asked, "Who's calling?"

A voice at the other end answered. "It's me, Carmen. I think I have good news. I explained to my wife, Chris, your frustration with not being able to locate your uncle. Remember I told you she's working at this home for the aged called Dumpsters in Tannersville?"

"Yes, I remember you telling me that."

"Well, she's uncertain whether or not it's your uncle, but there's a 93-year-old resident living there who fits his description."

"You're not pulling my leg, are you, Carmen?"

"No! It may be just coincidence, but his name is the same as your uncle's, Luigi Fettuccine. Maybe you should check it out."

"Thanks Carmen, I'll make sure I do."

"Glad to help," replied Carmen, "Good luck!"

Excited over this newly found information, Sonny let out a yelp, grabbed hold of his wife, and relayed the good news to her. Jo gave her elated husband a great big kiss and said, "Welcome back, stranger, you'll never know how much I've missed you."

Jumping with joy, Sonny said, "First thing in the morning I'm going to Dumpsters. As for tonight, let's celebrate. Break out the Asti!"

Bright and early the following morning, after a somewhat restless night twisting and turning, Sonny hopped out of bed and jumped in the shower.

After dressing and eating a quick breakfast, he got into his car and drove to Dumpsters.

The 20-minute drive seemed like an eternity. As he approached the facility, his eyes filled up. He thought, "Can it be true, my yearlong search is finally coming to an end?"

Sonny parked the car and hurried up the path leading to the front entrance. As he approached the large glass doors, they slid open. Once inside, he registered his name in the guest book and then checked the directory. There, in plain sight, was the familiar name, Luigi Fettuccine, Room 424, 2nd Floor. Once on the elevator, he hesitated and then pressed the button. As the doors opened, Sonny exited. Immediately adjacent to the elevator was the nurse's station. One of the nurses on duty asked if she could be of assistance.

"I'm here to see Mr. Fettuccine," said Sonny.

The staff members smiled. It just so happened that the director of nursing, Ms. Turnbuckle, was making rounds. She answered in a pleasant voice, "You mean Louie. He's in the lounge, third door on your left. Look for the guy with the big smile, probably telling jokes to the rest of the residents."

Sonny offered his thanks and proceeded down the hall. Sure enough, there he was. This 93-year-old, somewhat handsome gentleman was joking with his friends. His resemblance to Sonny was incredible. His stature was that of a much younger man. Unable to contain his anxiety another moment, Sonny entered the lounge. As he drew closer, the older man turned, smiled, and said, "Hello, Sonny."

Sonny was dumbfounded. It was truly uncanny how someone he hasn't seen for over fifty years was immediately able to identify him. Groping for the right words, he said, "Fettuccine, Luigi Fettuccine?"

"In the flesh, my boy. Come; let's go to my room. See you later, gang; this is my nephew. We have a few things to discuss."

As they walked down the corridor to Louie's room, Sonny couldn't help notice how spry his gait was.

Upon entering the room, the two men offered each other a long overdue embrace. Their eyes teared and their voices hushed. Sonny thought, "I've finally found Uncle Louie, the missing link in my family's heritage."

They sat down and exchanged small talk. Louie apologized for not returning after the war. "Please forgive me?" he asked.

"Of course, Uncle Louie, but there is no need to apologize. We're family."

"We certainly have a great deal of lost time to make up," Louie said.

"That's for sure. So many questions need answering. I want to gather as much information regarding my family history as possible. Mama always said, 'If you want your car fixed, go to a body shop and they'll straighten it out, but when you want your life straightened out, speak to Uncle Louie.' That's what I intend to do. Would you mind if I made weekly visits and we talked?"

"Certainly not, Sonny. Come whenever you like. I've been here two years. I'm not going anywhere, at least not yet."

Rising to his feet, Sonny said, "That's a deal, Uncle Louie. Now you must excuse me, I promised my wife I'd take her to dinner. Good-bye, I'll see you next week."

"So long, Sonny. I'll be waiting."

As Sonny departed, he gazed at the heavens and whispered, "Thank you dear Lord." He climbed into his car and drove off. During the drive home, he couldn't help noticing Mother Nature's artwork. Because of the all-encompassing thought of finding his uncle, he never paid attention to what was happening around him. Now with that under his belt, his spirits were on cloud nine.

Chapter 2
What Was He Like?

As Sonny pulled into the driveway, Jo stood anxiously waiting. When she spotted the car, she hurried down the steps to greet him. "Sonny," she said, "what was your uncle like? Was he friendly? Did he have all his faculties?"

"Slow down, Jo," he said. "Try to control your emotions 'til we get in the house."

Once inside, they sat down. Once again she continued. "Well, tell me, what was he like?"

"What was who like?"

"That's it. Now you've done it." As she opened the closet door, she said, "Where the heck's Robert's baseball bat?"

"Come on, Jo, can't you take a joke? Sit down and relax."

"Relax?" said Jo. "Relax? I've been on pins and needles all day waiting for your return."

"Okay," Sonny answered. "Wait 'til I get a beer. I'm dying of thirst."

Jo waited patiently as she watched him open the refrigerator door, grab a cold beer, and open it. In the meantime, she was making buttons.

As he sat down, Sonny began, "Jo, I wish you had been there to meet him. I'm certain you'd feel the same. I never thought I'd meet someone exactly like me."

"You mean a pain in the ass!" said Jo.

"Thanks," said Sonny, continuing. "He's 20 years my senior, but because of his mannerisms, you wouldn't know it."

"Does he resemble your mother or your father?"

"Neither," replied Sonny. "As a matter of fact, you might say I resemble *him*."

"Really? Please," Jo begged, "tell me everything."

"O.K., if you insist," he winked. "Here goes. I never realized what a beautiful facility Dumpsters is. As many times as I've passed, I had no inkling what existed beyond the high stone wall. Of course, that's true of many things. Only when directly affected, as in this case, are they of any consequence. Now, let's see, certain parts of the building must be every bit of 150 years old, though well maintained."

Yawning, Jo interrupted. "What about Uncle Louie?"

"Hold your horses, I'll get to that in a minute. After all, you did ask me to tell everything. Now, where was I? Oh yes! The grounds were immaculate. Hedge groves surrounded a variety of flowers. My nostrils filled with the smell of freshly cut grass. Throughout the inside perimeter of the stone wall, deciduous trees gently blew in the warm breeze. In closer proximity to the main building, specimen trees were planted. Running along the sidewalk up to the entrance, Alberta spruce lined the way, interspersed with colorful azalea bushes."

At that point, Sonny noticed Jo's eyes rolling in boredom. Sonny continued with his explicit description. "As I approached the entrance, the large glass sliding doors parted. I entered and couldn't help noticing how everything, including the mirrors, sparkled." Sonny failed to see Jo's eyes had closed as she entered into a deep slumber. Undeterred, he went on and on, giving every last detail. "Unlike some facilities, this was immaculate, with not the least hint of an odor or loud distraction."

Just then, Jo let out a snore that rocked the room. Sonny called, "Jo, wake up! You're snoring. You didn't hear a word I said."

"I did too, I'm not snoring! You're just saying that. Come now, don't stop; don't leave me hanging…"

"Well I'll be," said Sonny. "The best way to describe Uncle Louie is to say there is a strong family resemblance between us. He's approximately five feet nine, and weighs about 175 pounds. His skin tone is light, and his gray hair is thinning. A Roman nose is the centerpiece of his face. He has perfectly-shaped lips and beady brown eyes. His ears stay close to his perfectly-shaped head." Sonny continued, "The upper torso is well-formed, leading me to believe he continues to do some physical exercise. His lower extremities are thin and slightly bowed. He is intelligent, quick of wit, and has a strong command of the English language. He is also well-versed in Italian. I guess that's about it, Jo," Sonny concluded as he turned to find her dozing once again.

"How do you like that?" Sonny thought to himself. "She's sound asleep." Rising from his chair, he went into the kitchen, dropped the empty bottle into the recycling bin, and then returned to the living room to awaken

Sleeping Beauty. He tapped her gently to arouse her, reminding her of their dinner engagement with their good friends, Colista and John.

Jo sat up and asked, "What do you mean, 'wake up'? I *am* awake."

"Oh, that's good," said Sonny. "Then I won't have to repeat the outcome of my meeting with Uncle Louie, isn't that so?"

"You're absolutely right. I heard every word."

"In that case, we'd better get a move on or we'll be late for dinner."

After getting ready, they got into the car and left to meet their friends. Soon after parking, they entered the restaurant, where they found Colista and John anxiously waiting.

The maitre d' showed them to their table. When seated he asked, "Is this the first time you've dined here?"

"No," said John, "but we came back anyway." The poor fellow, at a loss for words, turned red. Smiling, John said, "Just kidding," to the relief of everyone.

Sonny asked, "How have you two been?"

"Great!" John replied. "We've had a busy week."

"Really?" asked Sonny.

"Yes," replied Colista. "Every day this past week was spent at the doctor's office for either blood work or x-ray exams. Thank God the results were favorable."

"That's good, Colista," said Sonny. "I'm not looking forward to next week. I have an appointment with a *rear admiral*. I'm having a colonoscopy."

John laughed and said, "By the way, Sonny, how did your visit with your uncle turn out?"

"Yes," said Colista. "Tell us about it."

Sonny stole a glance at Jo, noting the elevation of her eyebrows and the muffled sigh she let out. Taking a cue from her expression, he said, "I'm so darned hungry. Why don't we wait 'til dinner's over? It's a long story."

On that note, while peering at the ceiling, Jo blessed herself.

During the course of the evening, the couples laughed, joked, and enjoyed a rapturous dining experience. While the two men sat waiting for their wives to return from the little girls' room, they continued their conversation. "Did you hear about the local official who was recently released from prison?"

"What was he in for?" asked John.

"According to the paper," Sonny explained, "misappropriation of funds, among other things. You're not going to believe this; he's thinking of making a career change."

"What's he up to this time?" John queried.

"He plans on becoming a financial planner."

John damn near choked on his coffee. "Here come the girls now. Guess it's time to go."

After paying the tab, they exited the restaurant and went out to the parking lot. Chatting along the way, Jo said, "I'll call Tuesday, Colista, to make arrangements for our trip to Atlantic City."

"Sounds good to me, Jo," she replied.

After saying farewell, they entered their cars for the drive home. As they pulled out of the parking lot, Sonny said, "Doggone it, I forgot to tell them about Uncle Louie. I'll have to call soon as we get home."

"Can't it wait 'til tomorrow?" Jo asked. "It's quite late. I'm sure they'll be tired when they get home. Besides, I don't feel like rehashing your description of Dumpsters over again."

Avoiding a chance for confrontation, Sonny reluctantly agreed.

After arriving home, they retired for the evening.

The following day, Sonny received a call from Ms. Turnbuckle, inquiring as to whether he could drive his uncle to the doctor's office. After agreeing, the next morning, he stopped at Dumpsters to pick up Louie. Upon reaching the dermatologist's office, they entered the waiting room, where they waited for Louie's appointed time. Louie was surprised to find all the chairs occupied by older men. He closed his eyes while Sonny picked up a magazine. A half hour passed, when Louie decided to approach the receptionist's desk, "Pardon me," he said, "am I in the wrong place?"

"Why do you ask?" she said.

"Oh, I was just wondering if I had walked in on someone's bachelor party?"

"Bachelor party!" she said. "What makes you think that?"

"I guess," said Louie, "because the last time I saw a bunch of guys watching a *skin flick*, I was at one."

"Sir! For your information," she said, "that's a closed circuit infomercial. She's a professional model physically describing the rudiments of examining the breast."

Caught off guard, Louie said, "Times certainly have changed. When last I saw a broad feeling herself up that way, I was watching the X-rated movie, *Debbie Does Dallas.*"

Exasperated, the receptionist said, "Sir! As I explained, the model is demonstrating how to properly examine the breast."

"Young lady," said Louie, "those old geezers are beyond the examination phase.

From the way they're drooling, they're about to get it on any minute!"

Suddenly realizing he had dozed off, when hearing his name he jumped from the chair. Apologizing to the nurse for daydreaming, he was shown to an examining room, told to strip, and wait for the doctor. As the door opened, Louie stood in his Johnny coat, surprised to learn Dr. Foreskin was female. There was one other thing of note; her resemblance to the girl of his dreams was remarkable.

Smiling, the good doctor asked, "So Mr. Fettuccine, what seems to be on your mind?"

Hesitating, Louie said, "Don't go there, Doc!"

While Louie was having a lesion excised from his thigh, Sonny remained in the waiting room. As he watched patients being called, he noticed the unprofessional manner used to acknowledge them. Shouting out a patient's name left a lot to be desired. That's when it hit him. *What an innovative idea,* he thought; *I can hardly wait to tell Jo.*

When Louie's minor surgical procedure was completed, Sonny drove him back to Dumpsters. After leaving, he headed home. Rushing into the house, Sonny began calling for Jo. She came flying down the stairs.

"What happened?"

"Take it easy Jo, nothing happened, I just wanted to tell you my terrific idea," he said.

"Gosh, I wish you wouldn't do that. You nearly gave me a heart attack," she said.

"What's the big deal, anyway?"

"Hear me out. When a customer visits a restaurant, once registered, they're handed a pager. Do you recall the time we ate at the Outback? We were given one. When it vibrated, we knew our table was ready," said Sonny.

"Yes I do."

"I think the same system can be used in a doctor's office. For example, most waiting rooms are overcrowded and stuffy. Not only that, the magazines are from year one."

"I'll say," said Jo.

"With the use of a pager," said Sonny, "you would have the freedom to exit the building and take a stroll. As your appointment time draws near, the office would send out a signal to your pager, which in turn would vibrate, alerting you to return."

"What a *great* idea!" said Jo.

"On my way home I contacted the franchiser on my cell phone," said Sonny, "I'm waiting for a call back." Just then the phone rang. "That's probably the company returning my call." Picking up the receiver, Sonny answered.

After a lengthy conversation, he hung up.

"Who called?" said Jo. "Was it the paging company?"

"Yes," said Sonny. "They said, a customer must purchase a minimum of 25 units. In addition, they would need to have their own transmitter."

"Are you thinking of buying a franchise and starting your own business?" asked Jo.

"That's what I had in mind. That is until, they explained the costs would run around 3,000 dollars," he said. "If I were to tack on a five percent commission, having worked with doctors for the better part of my life, they'd most likely pass on it."

"What's the bottom line?" asked Jo.

"I decided to close shop and go back into retirement," said Sonny.

"Thank God!" she said, "It's almost time for *Everybody Loves Raymond.*"

The next day, Sonny stopped by to see how Louie was feeling following surgery. When he arrived, he found him and a friend sitting on the porch. Before Sonny had a chance to ask how he was, Louie said, "I'd like you to meet my friend, Herman."

After acknowledging one another, Louie continued, "We have something important to tell you. Wait 'til you hear what we learned this morning."

"Regarding what?" Sonny asked.

"The history of the Dumpstir family," Louie said. "Phinius Dumpstir VI, a descendant of the founder, was here earlier to speak to the residents."

"It was very interesting," said Herman.

"Would you like to hear about it?" asked Louie.

"Yes I would," said Sonny.

"Phinius Dumpstir, born in 1789, the grandson of Commodore Cornelius Dumpstir, was the founder of Dumpstir's Home for the Insane. Dumpstirs was constructed sometime between 1825 and 1830. The original name has been changed. The name Dumpstir is a compound of dump and stir. *Dump* being a poorly maintained or disreputable place, and *Stir*, the British slang for prison. Dumpstirs opened to the public in 1830."

"Uncle Louie, when did the name change come about?" asked Sonny.

"I'll get to that in a minute," said Louie.

"Dumpstirs originally was built to be a *loony bin*," said Herman.

"Hush, Herman," said Louie. "Someone might overhear you."

"So what, it's the truth," said Herman. "It was nothing more than a *booby hatch.*"

"Even so," said Louie. "You don't have to go around advertising."

"Please continue, Uncle Louie," said Sonny.

"Originally it was said Dumpstirs was built by Phinius to house his mother, who was mentally deranged," said Louie.

"He means she was a screwball!" said Herman. Louie turned with eyebrows raised to look at Herman, then continued.

"The building we're standing in wasn't completed for some time. The sad part was, just previous to its completion, his mother committed suicide. Though never proven, there was a possibility of foul play."

"Yeah!" said Herman. "I bet Phinius's wife shoved the old lady out the window."

"Okay, Sherlock Chan, if that's the case," said Louie, "explain why Mrs. Dumpstir was completely exonerated?"

"Quite simple, my dear Holmes. Her attorney, Giovanni Cookooroni played the nut card," said Herman.

"If I didn't know better, I'd think you were nuts," said Louie. "The truth of the matter is, as in many cases, Mrs. Dumpstir's death was never resolved. With regard to the name change, years ago, placing a family member in an institution was frowned upon. Therefore the facility remained vacant. It wasn't until 1832, while on the verge of bankruptcy, Phinius turned to another source for help. Pettibone Placement, founder of the first placement agency in America, came to the rescue."

"That guy," said Herman, "was nutty as a fruitcake."

Once again disregarding Herman's derogatory innuendo, Louie continued. "Fruitcake, I mean Placement! See now Herman, you got me all screwed up!"

"Pardon me," said Herman. Louie then continued.

"Placement claimed that if the name was changed from Dumpstirs to Dumpsters, every bed would be occupied within a year. Furthermore, he guaranteed the first bed would be filled within a month's time. He promised that if he was unable to meet his commitment, no money needed to be exchanged. As was customary in those days, a handshake sealed the bargain."

"What was the outcome?" asked Sonny.

"In order to honor his obligation," said Louie, "Placement worked tirelessly. The stress he placed upon himself was enormous. Finally, after exhausting all avenues, with time running out, he fulfilled his pledge."

"Fruitcake went screwy," said Herman.

"Will you please shut up, Herman," said Louie.

"Placement went insane. His wife had him committed to the newly-named Dumpsters, thus fulfilling his prophecy to fill the first bed within a month's time."

Left with his mouth open, Sonny looked at Louie, who in turn eyeballed Herman. The two masters of the con began laughing, momentarily joined by Sonny after having the wool pulled over his eyes.

Chapter 3
A Day at the Races

The ensuing days flew. Jo left for her dental appointment early Wednesday morning. Shortly after breakfast, Sonny left for Dumpsters. As luck would have it, his car broke down. He called a service to have the vehicle towed to the dealership. Once the inspection was complete, the service manager determined the problem stemmed from a faulty computer chip. Agreeing to leave the car, Sonny was given a loaner and soon was back on the road. He parked the car in the lot and entered Dumpsters to find Louie and a few friends engaged in a discussion. He couldn't help noticing Louie holding a fistful of dollars.

As soon as Louie's companions noticed Sonny standing in the doorway, they apprised him of his nephew's presence. Turning, Louie smiled and gestured Sonny over, gave him a hug, then introduced him to his cohorts. After a friendly exchange, Louie placed his arm around Sonny's shoulder as they proceeded to his room. Passing a doorway, he motioned to Sonny, whispering, "This is my lady friend's room. What a gorgeous doll she is. Her name is Mamie. We've been keeping company for about six months, and have fallen in love." As they passed a door marked *Hazardous Material*, Sonny asked, "What's behind that door?"

"*Shitty diapers,*" said Louie.

Once inside Louie's room, they sat down. Sonny asked, "Were you booking horses?"

"Me?" he said. "No way. I'll have nothing to do with those unpredictable nags."

"What was that money you were holding?" asked Sonny.

"You mean this?" Louie asked as he pulled a wad of singles from his pocket. "These were the bets they placed on yesterday's race."

"By chance, did I hear correctly, the money you're holding is from racing bets? If your friends were not betting on horses, then what were they betting on?"

"Wheelchair races," said Louie.

"Wheelchair races!" exclaimed Sonny. "You mean to say they bet on wheelchair races?"

"That's right," said Louie, "But due to a terrible accident, the race was called off."

"Would you mind explaining?" asked Sonny. "But first tell me, who did you have your money on?"

"Me?" said Louie. "I haven't gambled since Hollywood fixed the chariot race in *Ben Hur.* Today, all races are fixed, even the one for the moon. I prefer being an odds maker and holding bets. Gambling's for suckers. By the way, where was I? Oh yes. Babs, one of our residents, was a former racecar driver. One day at Cocomo Raceway, she was involved in a six-car collision. Since that incident, she's become a wheelchair driver. Babs is one tough cookie. She took her lumps and never cried *uncle.* Two months ago, she came up with a great concept based on NASCAR; she calls it *NAPCHAIR* racing. The idea struck her one day while sitting in her wheelchair, waiting to have lunch. Babs noticed the anxiety of the residents awaiting entry into the dining room. I'll try to explain the outcome of her research.

"It's common knowledge that as lunchtime approaches, nursing home residents awaiting entry to the cafeteria suddenly awaken from their stupor. They begin jockeying for position. Their moves mimic those associated with racecar drivers, anticipating the start of competition. Excited, participants grasp their wheels, as adrenaline begins to pump. The odds-on favorite to capture the winner's pole in this morning's race was Bertha Biggs, better known in racing circles as 'Big Bertha.' According to consensus, the 400-pound darling was a cinch to take the pole.

"Those in the know felt the competition would find it extremely difficult to maneuver around Biggs's flank, giving her a leg-up."

"How many entries were there?" asked Sonny.

"I believe 15 in all, including Big Bertha, Hot Rod Rodney, Dick Furst, Freddie Fish, and Castrovitabellanote. With less then a minute to go, the cafeteria doors flung open," continued Louie. "The manager stepped into the hallway to take the lunchtime head count. Accidentally dropping her checkered napkin, Ms. Pratt bent over to retrieve it. Believing it to be the starting signal, Dick Furst lunged forward, rear ending an unsuspecting *Pratt.*

"As the rest of the pack scrambled for position, all hell broke lose. Freddie Fish pitted himself after losing a wheel. Immediately, Herman, the crew chief, and his contingent tried replacing it to no avail. It seems someone's bridgework, missing since last week, became entangled in the spokes. Fish raised a stink with the official."

"Who officiated?" Sonny asked.

"I did," said Louie.

"What happened next?" asked Sonny.

"For some reason, Biggs—slow to start—began to make her move. Extremely aroused, Dick pulled out from behind, thrusting in front. Pratt was spared further screw-up, by the *quick action of the staff.*

"After negotiating the hairpin curves, Dick went limp. Avoiding a now-listless Dick, the remainder of the pack began colliding into the walls, banging one another.

"Unbeknownst to the crowd, Big Bertha took the unchallenged lead. Unfortunately, within several yards of the finish line, she hit a grease slick from a bacon spill, causing her to spin out. In doing so, she ruptured her tank. As gas began leaking, an overpowering stench filled the air. Then the unimaginable happened," said Louie. "Her chair capsized as it flung through space, lodging between the doorjambs. Only by the grace of God, and the good sense to wear restraints, was she kept from being thrown. Overwrought, Bertha began to lose it, most likely from failing to make a pit stop.

"Spectators watched in horror as emergency crews arrived on the scene. While police cordoned off a 25-foot radius adjacent to the site of the accident, firefighters locked the Jaws of Life in place. The news media was on hand. As usual, state and local officials made an appearance; elections were just around the corner. As the crowd began to mount, a carnival-like atmosphere prevailed.

"Working feverishly, rescuers were able to extricate Bertha without incident. When free, a TV anchorperson asked Bertha, 'After such a horrible experience, will you enter next year's competition?' 'You betcha!' snarled Biggs, pumping her fist, 'I'll never say uncle!' The anchorperson asked, 'Do you have any thoughts as to what went wrong?' Big Bertha replied, 'Not really. I just thank God I'm still here to talk about it. I'm a competitor. I've been one since childhood. Growing up in a family with seven brothers taught me that. You may find it hard to believe by looking at me,' she chuckled, 'but I was always first at the dinner table. My dear mother, may she rest in peace, was built exactly like me. She instilled in me my competitive nature.' About then, Doctor Feelfine interrupted to say, 'Thank you ladies and gentlemen.

I think that's enough questions for now. Ms. Biggs needs some rest.' As we began to depart the area, Bertha was whisked away, shouting to her fans, 'I'll be back! I'll never say uncle!'"

Leaving Louie's room, they headed in the direction of the dining area. After arriving, Sonny pointed out the visible damage to the doorframe.

"Most of the damage must be attributable to the Jaws of Life," said Sonny.

"I'm sure you're right. Come, let's go in, I'll show you our table," said Louie.

Because the room was empty, Sonny couldn't help notice the table settings. There was a small vase of daisies in the center; the napkins, glassware, and silverware were neatly arranged, along with name cards.

"Over here Sonny. This is our table by the window. I asked for an ocean view, but in the Pocono Mountains, that's next to impossible. Take a look out the window. See the birdbath? That's the best they could do."

As Sonny peered out, Louie continued, "Look, there's Tony the handyman digging around." Louie rapped on the window, trying to get his attention. "Tony! Tony!" he called. As Tony acknowledged, Louie said, "Save a nice spot next to the birdbath for me."

Tony smiled as he gave Louie a thumbs-up.

Sonny's attention returned to the table. "I notice Mamie, Sally, and Herman sit with you."

Louie nodded in agreement. "We've got a great table, a nice view, and good company to boot. Best of all, every day we have a private show."

"What do you mean by a private show?" asked Sonny

"Do you remember me telling you that Sally and Herman are retired circus performers?"

"Yes," said Sonny, "I do."

"Every time we sit down to eat, they go into their act. First Herman goes over to the closet, removes their special booster seats, and puts them in place. Then he takes Sally by the arm and says, 'Madame, your chariot awaits.' He squats in a knee/chest position as Sally steps on to his back. Then Herman mumbles, 'Sally, my dear, you must cut a few calories.' That comment is her cue to sit down. Herman rises slowly, crying, 'Oh, my aching back!'"

"That's cute," Sonny laughed.

"Ah, the best is yet to come. Once we're seated and ready to eat, Herman places his water glass alongside his right elbow." Louie gestured emphatically as he explained.

"Next, Herman moves to cut his meat, accidentally knocking over the glass, spilling water onto Sally's lap. The sweet little lady says, 'Herman, my love, would it not make more sense to place your water glass in front of your plate, out of the way?' Herman answers in his upper-class Scottish brogue, 'Sally, my sweet, if I were to do as you suggest, it would preclude any chance of my knocking it onto your lap.'"

"Aw, Uncle Louie, are you sure it's only an act?"

Louie scratched his head and replied, "You know something Sonny? Now that you mention it, I've noticed lately Sally looking at the ceiling, rolling her big brown eyes."

"By the way, Uncle Louie, what kind of reaction have you gotten from your lady friend, Mamie?"

"A very positive one, she kicks me under the table." He raised his trouser to show Sonny the bruises. Continuing, Louie said, "Before you can say 'Castrovitabellanote,' the two of us burst out laughing so loudly, it resounds throughout the entire dining room. Not knowing why, most likely because of our heartfelt jubilation, the rest of the residents join in the laughter, followed by an explosive round of applause."

"You expect me to believe this is an ongoing occurrence?"

"Absolutely," responded Louie, "don't accept my word. Come see for yourself. As a matter of fact, we're occasionally allowed dinner guests. I'll get approval from Social Services and let you know. That way, you'll be able to draw your own conclusion."

Sonny paused, and then said, "Sounds good to me. I'm looking forward to it." Glancing at the wall clock, he said, "Uncle Louie, I see there's ample time before lunch. Would you mind if we return to the privacy of your room to discuss my heritage and the good old days?"

"Certainly, my boy. I'd be happy indeed to reminisce with you."

The two rose from their chairs to leave the dining room. Louie stopped to speak to one of the kitchen crew. "What's for lunch, Bessie?"

"Barbequed chicken, cole slaw, and baked beans," the woman replied as she continued chopping the cabbage and carrots.

"Oh my," said Louie.

"What's the problem?" Sonny asked, a look of concern crossing his face.

"Nothing really. It's just that whenever we eat cole slaw and baked beans, the next day, the laundry workers have a hell of a time shaking the farts out of the sheets."

Sonny laughed and grabbed his uncle by the arm. As they proceeded down the hall, Louie asked if Sonny would drive him to the mall.

"I have to pick up a gift," said Louie. "Sally and Herman are celebrating their 50th anniversary."

"I'd also like to give them something," said Sonny. "What's appropriate for 50 years?"

"Let's see," said Louie. "25 is silver, 75's platinum and 50's gold."

"What's for 100?" asked Sonny.

"*Rust,*" said Louie, "rust!"

When they approached Louie's room, they found Wandering Olivia gathering a few of Louie's belongings.

"What's she doing, Uncle Louie?"

"Don't let her see you," Louie shushed his nephew as he whispered. "Olivia can't help herself. Before retiring, she spent 40 years in the navy assigned to counterintelligence. She thinks we're spies; she's gathering evidence."

"What will she do with the items she's taking?" asked Sonny.

"By tomorrow," said Louie, "everything will be back in place. Olivia is meticulous; she will not leave a single fingerprint."

"How come?" asked Sonny.

"Didn't you notice her wearing rubber gloves? She does the same thing in every room. Over the years, she screwed up once. She was caught wearing Big Bertha's oversized bloomers, which fell down as she walked into the dining room. Administration, though aware of her espionage tactics, allows her to continue."

"You've got to be kidding," said Sonny.

"No, I'm not. The other residents don't mind, it makes Olivia happy." As Olivia completed her mission, she slithered out of the room. Louie said, "Hello, Double O," as she vanished next door into Herman's room.

"How come you called her Double O?"

"Simple, her name is Olivia Oliphant. Get it?"

"Yes, I do," Sonny, replied.

Once they were seated, Louie began. "Enough of that. Let's see. Where shall I begin? Oh yes. My papa and mama were from southern Italy. I won't go into detail; that would complicate matters. I'll begin with Papa. He left his native Italy and arrived at Ellis Island. That's where immigrants were processed before entering the country. It was around the turn of the century when the influx of immigrants was constantly on the increase, as foreigners came to America to find the good life. Pre-arrangements were made as to where he would live until he was able to fend for himself. At the time, he was 16. He lived with the Paletta family for quite some time. They treated him as one of their own. From them, he learned family values, which were passed on to us.

"The house they lived in was a cold-water flat located in Orange, New Jersey. The only heat available was from a coal stove. In order to have hot water for bathing, they ignited a small gas-operated unit in the cellar. The flame would heat the coils, which in turn heated the pipes, producing hot water. Otherwise, cold water was always available. Are you following me?"

"Go on Uncle Louie," Sonny said.

"Mr. Paletta was friendly with one of the top salesmen at Swinger Sewing Machine Company. The man was kind enough to put in a good word for Papa, enabling him to land a sales position. The job was no cakewalk, but was one in which Papa excelled. It entailed a combination of good sales ability, strength, and determination. Papa had all three qualities, and then some.

"As a salesperson, he had to walk up two to three flights of stairs, lugging an 85-pound sewing machine, though he never complained. At night, while he lay in bed, many thoughts entered his mind. Going into business for himself was key. As a youngster in Italy, he worked as a tailor's apprentice. Papa learned how to design and make custom suits for himself. Soon his friends began asking where he got the suits. He explained that he made them. At first, no one believed him, but before long, they changed their minds. In fact, they began asking Papa to make suits for them. He obliged, for a price, of course."

Louie took a deep breath and then continued. "Word got around as additional orders continued to come in. He had his eye on a store; the price was within his means, and so he made the deal with the owner and purchased the location. He had his name, Emilio Fettuccine, imprinted on the plate glass. Orders flew in for Emilio's custom made suits. Business was booming, and soon after, he hired ten tailors to work for him. Wealthy individuals from the other side of town were placing orders, five or six at a time. It was unbelievable to think Papa, an immigrant from Italy, through hard work and determination, built a wonderful business.

"Mama came to America from Salerno, Italy at age six. Her family was close friends with Papa's family in Italy. Her father had money. When they arrived, he was able to buy a house. He also had the promise of employment from a relative who had lived in America for 15 years. Everything was working out wonderfully for Mama's family."

Louie stared at Sonny and said, "Now that I've laid the groundwork, Sonny, there's a piece of the puzzle that's missing."

Sonny, who had been listening attentively, stood up and walked over to his uncle. Placing a hand on his shoulder, he asked, "What might that be?"

"I'm unable to figure out how Mama and Papa met, although if I were to guess, I'd say their marriage had been prearranged in the old country. At the time of their marriage, Papa was 26 and Mama 16. In the meantime, Papa's business had grown considerably. Believe it or not, he yearned to own a small neighborhood grocery. I never knew why, but guess what? When someone made him an offer he couldn't refuse, he sold his lucrative tailor shop for a handsome price. He took the money and opened the business he had dreamed of; his very own grocery store.

"In the meantime, the Fettuccine family was growing. Aside from Mama and Papa, I had a wonderful brother and sister." A stream of tears trickled down Sonny's face at the mention of his mother.

"When were you born, Uncle Louie?" Sonny asked.

"On Thanksgiving Day, Papa's friends in jest would say, 'Emilio, I think your wife has a turkey in the oven.' I guess, Sonny, that's why at times I have a *fowl* mouth."

Sonny laughed gently patting his uncle on the back in appreciation. "Uncle Louie, you're a piece of work!"

"You're 100 percent right, Sonny."

They shared a good laugh. Then Sonny looked at the wall clock and said, "Well, Uncle Louie, I see it's almost lunchtime. I have to pick up my car at the dealership. I had a computer problem and they promised it would be ready today. I'll be back next week to continue our conversation."

Louie rose from his Morris chair. As they hugged, his bright eyes twinkling, he said, "I'll walk you to the front door. When I sit too long, my lumbago kicks in. I guess I'm starting to get old!"

As the two men left the room and walked down the brightly lit hallway, Louie said, "My stomach's beginning to gurgle. Must be close to lunch."

Sonny asked, "Do you think Sally and Herman will perform this afternoon?"

"Without a doubt! The show must go on."

They approached the front door and offered their farewells as Sonny departed. Louie waved good-bye and then walked off in the direction of Mamie's room. They were seldom apart. After meeting Louie outside her door, the two strolled hand-in-hand over to the dining room, to enjoy dinner and a show at the behest of Herman and Sally Short.

Chapter 4
Circus Mysteries

It was a steamy, overcast June day. Not caring to play golf, Sonny decided to put the finishing touches on the final piece of the miniature circus he made for his granddaughter, Erica. Starting from scratch, Sonny crafted his masterpiece.

The project, made from Styrofoam, was molded, formed, and glued together to replicate every detail of a three-ring circus, complete with the usual cast of performers found under the big top. Included were a variety of animals and circus acts. A band and clowns of every description were present. He garnered together a host of household items: cardboard, caps, wooden dowels, felt, and material left over from Jo's many projects. What was unavailable, he purchased from a local craft store.

Strung across the span of the trapeze towers was a banner inscribed with the name, ERICA'S BIG TOP CIRCUS. Tiny working searchlights mounted on stanchions played on the entire scope of the circus, illuminating it during evening performances. Located beneath the bandstand was a tiny recorder that played familiar songs usually associated with the buffoons of the circus, such as "Send in the Clowns." The smiling faces of an audience were painted on the backdrop. They seemed to be enjoying the many antics of the clowns.

As a reward for time expended, Sonny received gratification from the gleam in his grandchildren's eyes. Whenever they tell friends about it, they're filled with enthusiasm.

Just as Sonny finished straightening his workshop, the basement door flung open. Jo called down, "Honey, how much longer will you be?"

"I'll be up in a minute," he answered.

"Do you plan on seeing Uncle Louie? It's Wednesday."

"As a matter of fact, I am," he said while climbing the stairs. He walked into the kitchen, where Jo just finished putting away breakfast dishes.

"Would you mind dropping me off at Pleasant Valley Manor to see my mom?" she asked.

"Not at all," he answered. "First I must stop at the Jordans'. I want to drop off the final piece of Erica's circus." With the completion of the last little clown, the project was finished. Sonny's 350-hour labor of love was ready for its first performance.

After dropping Jo off, he left for Dumpsters. When he arrived, he found Louie standing out front talking to one of the employees. As Sonny walked over to Louie, he said, "Hi Sonny! I'd like you to meet Philip."

"Congratulations," Sonny said as they exchanged handshakes. "I understand you're to receive a special commendation for your part in the dramatic rescue of Big Bertha."

Humbly, Philip thanked him, said goodbye and walked inside. His superior had summoned him.

As he left, Louie said, "What a gentleman, and so modest. Sonny, acts of heroism are not new to Philly. He was assigned to one of the toughest units in the army—the 2nd Battalion, 23rd Infantry Division, under General Mathew Ridgeway. Those guys were responsible for driving North Koreans and their Chinese counterparts clear out of South Korea. I'm the only one who knows that Philly was presented with the Distinguished Service Cross. Talk about *never saying uncle*, you can bet there's a guy who won't."

"Come, Sonny," Louie continued. "I see the lounge is empty. Let's go in and talk." After sitting, Louie began dabbling on a word puzzle another resident had begun.

Louie asked, "How's the car running since you had it fixed?"

"Like a charm," said Sonny. "Uncle Louie, do you recall telling me Herman and Sally were retired circus performers?"

"Of course I do. Why do you ask?"

"I'm very interested in anything pertaining to the circus, especially the performers. As a matter of fact, just today I finished crafting a replica of a miniature circus for my granddaughter," said Sonny.

"Wow!" said Louie. "That must have taken a long time."

"It sure did," he said. Then Sonny explained the entire circus project to Louie. He described each performer in detail. As he looked down, he noticed Louie had been working on a crossword puzzle. "Have you finished?"

"Except for one word!" said Louie.

"What's that?" asked Sonny.

"What's a five letter word for buffoon?" asked Louie.

After pondering the question, Sonny said, "Clown."

Pausing a minute to check, Louie said, "Good! That'll work." Raising his head to thank him, Louie announced, "Speaking of clowns, here comes Herman now!"

"Hello fellows," said Herman, "what's happening?"

"Sonny was telling me about the circus he made for his granddaughter," said Louie. "Why don't you tell Sonny about your days under the big top."

"Would you, Herman?" asked Sonny. "I'm fascinated by stories about the circus." Without a moment's hesitation, proud of his former circus days, Herman started in.

"My first experience was as a roustabout, working for King Brothers' Circus, in Glasgow, Scotland."

"Aha!" said Sonny. "I thought I detected a wee bit of a Scottish brogue!"

"When Sally and I first met, she worked as a chanteuse at a nearby nightclub I frequented. Not long after meeting, we fell in love and later tied the knot. Sally and I both desired to become circus clowns. During off hours, we perfected a dynamic act. When Mr. King saw it, we were hired on the spot. He paid us 300 bucks a week. With the passing of time, the Shorts became headliners. Mr. John Dingaling, of Dingaling Brothers Farnum and Frailey, got wind of our act. We received a telegram from him with an offer."

"Tell Sonny how much Dingaling offered to pay you," said Louie.

"Okay, okay!" said Herman. "Give me a chance! At the time, he offered us the unheard-of sum of 10,000 smackeroos a week!"

"Wow!" said Sonny. "That's unbelievable, tell more."

"Let's see, oh yes," said Herman, "it was late 1942. After crossing the U-boat infested waters of the Atlantic aboard the Queen Elizabeth, we docked in New York Harbor. Dingaling himself, surrounded by an entourage of dignitaries, including the mayor and Cardinal Shaeen, were there to welcome us. After the greeting, we were whisked away in his private limo to the famous Talldorf Astoria, where a tumultuous welcome awaited. A party followed, attended by VIPs from all corners of the globe. A bountiful display of culinary delicacies adorned the beautifully decorated tables. The both of us had all to do to keep from pinching ourselves. On the terrace, adjacent to the dining room, a ten-piece society orchestra played melodies of love. I requested the orchestra to play one of my favorites, "Meditation." At party's end, we were taken to the presidential suite."

"My," said Sonny, "how exciting!"

"Wait," said Louie, "the best is yet to come. Go on, Herman, tell Sonny what happened next."

"Once inside our suite, I looked out the sliding glass doors. The view was breathtaking. To get a better perspective, Sally and I ventured onto the terrace. Against Sally's wishes, opting for a better vantage point, I climbed onto a ledge. As I stretched for still a better view, without warning, my footing gave way and over I went. In the background, I heard Sally screaming frantically. Down I tumbled, down, down, down 'til I abruptly crashed with a sickening thud."

"My goodness," said Sonny, "how awful. Were you badly injured?"

"No," said Herman, "with the exception of my pride."

"I don't understand," said Sonny.

"Well," said Herman, "how would you feel if you just fell out of bed and your wife was screaming, at the top of her lungs, 'Mr. King warned you the next time you're late for work, you'll be back shoveling *elephant dung!*'" The two old bozos held their breath, waiting to see Sonny's reaction. Rendered speechless, realizing he'd been duped, Sonny shook his head.

Regaining his composure, Sonny said, "What I'm about to tell you is a true story. Shortly past midnight, my daughter Joanne and her husband Anthony were awakened by the sound of music playing. It seemed to be coming from my granddaughter Erica's room. Upon closer inspection, the song they heard was 'Send in the Clowns.' It ended abruptly as they got out of bed to check. Befuddled, they got back in bed and fell off to sleep. At daybreak, they were roused by the sight of Erica standing in the doorway. In her hand, she held an object."

"What happened next?" asked Louie.

"Joanne asked her daughter what she was holding. Handing it to her mother, Erica said, 'an angel.' Upon closer inspection, Joanne flicked a switch and the tune 'Amazing Grace' began playing. Stopping it, she turned the tiny angel over noticing an inscription written on its base. It read, *To my little Angel from Nana Mary.* Overwrought, Joanne asked Erica to explain where she found the angel. To which Erica answered, 'I'm confused, Mommy.' Joanne asked what about. Erica explained that when she came home from school, she was happy to find I had finished the circus. The performers were all in place, with the exception of one little clown, which she found lying on the playroom floor. Erica said, 'I picked him up, noticing he felt wet; I wrapped him in a towel to dry.' Later she said, 'I brought the tiny clown to my bedroom and placed him on the nightstand.' She told her mother, that night she prayed for God to make him well. The following morning, when she awakened, she told her mother that in his place was the tiny musical angel."

"Wow," said Herman, "that's unbelievable. Go on, Sonny."

"The trio was interrupted by five-year-old Mark, who flew into the room wanting to know what was going on. At that point, Joanne told me she was stunned, explaining that it was the same angel given to her by *her* grandmother when she was three years of age. Furthermore, she told me that when she was seven, the angel disappeared and has been missing over 30 years."

"Missing for 30 years and it just showed up? Sure sounds strange to me!" said Louie.

"Wait, there's more," said Sonny. "Suddenly Joanne said she had a premonition. She asked Anthony to see if the paper had been delivered. While Anthony went to look, Joanne told me she and the kids went down to the playroom. She said while checking the circus characters, they found nothing disturbed, including the clown in question. At that point, Joanne said that Anthony came running down the steps holding the newspaper in his hand. As he began reading, he told of an incident that took place the night before.

"Apparently, he said, as the Klyde Weatie Circus crossed the Water Gap Bridge from New Jersey into Pennsylvania, a near tragedy was averted. It seems one of the clowns on a dare, while blindfolded, attempted to walk on the railing. In doing so, he slipped, plunging into the Delaware's icy waters. According to an eyewitness, suddenly the heavens overhead illuminated. From out of nowhere, a young girl with blonde flowing tresses swooped down. She grabbed hold of the clown twice her size; carrying him, she set him down on the shoreline. Sometime later, at Pocono Medical Center, when asked, the clown confirmed the eyewitness account. He added that in her hand, the young girl held a tiny angel, which played the tune 'Amazing Grace.'

"For crying out loud," said Herman, "was the clown crocked?"

"No," said Sonny emphatically. "According to the article, it remains a mystery."

"Then I suppose they'll never find out the true story," said Herman. Turning to Louie, he said, "What do you think?"

"One thing's for sure, the good Lord works in mysterious ways. I'm reminded of the day I received a call from you," Louie said as he pointed to Sonny.

"It must be a miracle," Herman said.

"Speaking of miracles," said Sonny, "if I don't get home soon, it'll be a miracle if Jo doesn't crown me. See you guys." He picked up and hastily left to go home.

Chapter 5
Scouting! That's a Good Thing

Sonny awakened just as the girls were pulling out of the driveway. Jo, Joanne, and Erica left to spend the day in New York to see the Broadway musical, *Annie Get Your Gun.* He began thinking of things to do.

Suddenly struck with an idea, he picked up the phone and called Louie to ask if he and his friend Herman would like to go fishing. While Sonny held on, Louie checked with Herman. When he returned, he said, "Yes, we'd like that very much."

Sonny told him to let Ms. Turnbuckle know he was taking them out for the day, to dress comfortably, and to be out front by 10:00 a.m. After hanging up, Sonny called his son Bob, who had the day off. Knowing him to be an avid angler, Sonny asked if he would like to join them. In response, Bob gave a definitive yes. "Bring two extra poles for the boys and be at my house by 9:00 a.m.," said Sonny. In the meantime, he got his gear together.

When Bob arrived, they packed the Jeep and left for Dumpsters to pick up Louie and Herman. The boys were waiting on the bench out front. They got out of the Jeep and walked over to where they were sitting.

"Hi fellas," Sonny said. "Meet my son, Bob. He's driving us."

Bob shook hands with Herman then turned to Louie. As he did, Louie said, "So this is my grand-nephew. Come, give your old uncle a hug."

Sonny said, "I hope you don't mind riding in a Jeep; we thought you might enjoy it. Bob took the top down."

"Are you kidding?" Herman said. "This'll be great!" Trying to reach the high step, Herman raised his foot in vain. After several attempts, refusing any assistance, he said, "I'll be back in a minute."

Louie said, "He's very independent. Herman's been on his own most of his life, performing in the circus. He'll figure out a way of getting in. As for me, Bob, I'll take all the help I can get."

Just as Bob finished helping Louie into the Jeep, they heard the whirring sound of an engine. Sure enough, rounding the corner of the building was the forklift with Phil at the controls, and Herman propped on top. As the machine drew closer, we wondered what their next move would be. Our question was soon answered. As Herman held tight, Phil raised the forklift, maneuvering it over the Jeep. Then, in typical circus tradition, Herman flipped, landing in Louie's lap.

Upset, Louie reached into his pocket, pulling out two smashed eggs. Holding them in his hand, he said, "Now look what you've gone and done. The cook hard-boiled them special for me. Darn you Herman! Every time you decide to perform, whether I like it or not, I end up in your act."

"Sorry Louie, guess I'm getting old." As Herman slid off Louie's lap, Bob and Sonny had all to do to keep from laughing.

Bob suggested Big Pocono State Park or Brady's Lake. "I know some good spots where we can catch native brookies."

"Sounds good to me," said Herman. "How about you, Louie?"

"To be honest, I had something else in mind," he said. "When I was a kid, my best friend and I found a great spot in Stillwater, New Jersey. Boy, if I could fish that lake again, I'd give a week's pay."

"But Louie," said Herman, "you're retired."

"I know, but if I were still on the payroll, that's what I'd do," he said.

"Uncle Louie, keep your money," Bob said. "Tell me how to get there."

A smile immediately crossed his face. "Take Route 80 East to Route 206 North in New Jersey. Travel about six to eight miles until you come to Old Scout Road. Make a right and travel up the hill about three miles. From that point, it's a short walk in."

"OK guys," said Bob, "hang onto your hats. First I must stop at Rudy's Bait and Tackle Shop to pick up some mealworms and shiners."

Once back in the Jeep, they set out for Route 80. Sonny and Bob were flabbergasted as to how precise Louie's recollection of the directions was, after not having been there for over 75 years. They parked the Jeep, gathered their gear, and began the short trek through the woods.

Suddenly Louie stopped. Bob asked if he was tired. "I'm fine," he answered. "Come fellas, take a look at this old oak tree." Carved into the bark were the initials L.F. and L.R.

Sonny asked, "Whose initials are L.R.?"

"A dear friend from my old neighborhood in Orange, New Jersey." he answered.

Bob said, "They really held up after all these years. Let's get going before it gets later."

After several hundred paces, they were surprised to find a heavy chain strung across the path. The sign hanging from it read, *Private Camp - Members Only.*

Upset, Louie was first to speak. "That's a fine kettle of fish. Turn your back one minute and out of nowhere somebody comes along and takes over."

"Wait a minute Louie, don't get your bowels in an uproar," said Herman.

"He's right," said Sonny. "There has to be a logical explanation."

"I see a large cabin ahead. Let's check it out," said Bob.

Posted on the cabin door was a plaque inscribed, *Troop 18. Mr. Richie, headmaster.* The foursome entered the cabin. Seated behind a large desk was a gentleman fingering through a pile of papers. He looked up and said, "I'm Mr. Richie. May I assist you?"

Quite peeved, Louie said, "What's the big idea? This was my old fishing spot. When did you guys move in?"

"Hold it a minute," Sonny said. "I'm sorry, Mr. Richie. I'd like to explain. My uncle fished here years ago and can't accept the fact that it's a private camp."

"That's quite all right. I'm sorry, but I didn't get your names," said Mr. Richie.

"I'm Sonny, this is Louie, Herman, and my son, Bob."

"Please allow me to explain. The campsite, including the lake, occupies 200 acres. The property belongs to Troop 18. In 1956, the land was willed to the troop in the Coldsore family's estate. Ever since, it's been operated as a camp. Is there some way I can assist you?" he asked.

"Yes," said Louie. "We want to go fishing."

"I'm afraid that would be impossible. You see it's for members only. By chance were either of you a Wolf or Eagle?"

"No," said Louie.

"Tenderfoot?" Mr. Richie asked.

"Come to think of it," said Herman, "both feet get a little tender. Most likely it's gout."

"No, no," said Mr. Richie. "Let me put it another way. Have either of you participated in any scouting activities?"

"Yes," said Louie, "when I was younger, I was involved in *girl scouting.*"

"Girl scouting? I'm confused. Would you mind explaining?"

"Sure. When I was in high school, my buddies and I drove around town trying to pick up girls; you know, girl scouting," said Louie.

"Oh I see," said Mr. Richie. "I'm sorry, girl scouting as defined in our manual has an altogether different meaning."

"What must Herman and I do to join?" Louie asked.

"Would you mind telling your ages?" asked Mr. Richie.

"Herman's just a kid, he's 86. I'm 93."

"Let me make a phone call. While I'm doing so, you're welcome to look around."

"If it's o.k. with you, we'll sit and wait, right guys?" They all agreed.

As they entered into a discussion amongst themselves, the headmaster made his call. After a brief conversation, he set the phone down and turned to his guests. "Gentlemen I have good news. Except for a few specifics, the central office will forgo most of the prerequisites."

"That's wonderful," said Sonny. "By the way, what are the requirements?"

Mr. Richie said, "First they must fill out the necessary forms, which include the usual: name, date, age, residence, etc. In addition, they must wear uniforms while in camp."

"Uniforms, you must be kidding! I haven't worn one since the war," said Louie.

"I'm sorry, but national headquarters insists upon it."

"Louie, don't be an old fogy," said Herman. "I think we'll look sharp."

"So do we," echoed Sonny and Bob as they embraced him.

Convinced, Louie said, "I'll do it. Where can we pick up the uniforms?" he asked.

"As soon as we leave here, on the way back to Dumpsters we can stop off at Dinklehoofers. They stock sporting goods. I'm sure we'll find uniforms there," said Sonny.

"By the way, gentlemen," said Mr. Richie, "there are a couple of minor obligations you must fulfill. First you must learn the troop pledge, secondly you must perform a good deed. Other than that, here are the manuals and registration forms." Handing them to Sonny, he said, "Have them fill out the necessary information and drop them off when they return."

After shaking hands they left the headmaster's office, got into the Jeep, and headed back to Pennsylvania, straight to Dinklehoofers. Once inside, they explained their needs to a salesperson. They were directed to the proper department.

They tried on uniforms, opting for summer wear. In the final analysis, it must be said, if they were standing alongside the more than one million troops worldwide, it would be difficult to tell them apart.

They were tickled when Herman said, "You know Louie I think we look pretty damn good. I'm going to have a talk with headmaster Richie. Did you hear the way he rattled off the oath?"

"Yes," said Louie, "How about the fruit salad he was wearing? Notice his Silver Beaver Award?"

"Smiling, Herman said, "Makes you wonder who Mr. Richie kissed up to in order get his *Beaver* award."

"Okay guys, we can leave now. Dinklehoofers gave us a senior discount," said Sonny.

"The hell with the senior discount," said Louie jokingly. "I'd rather be young again."

Laughing, Sonny said, "Well anyway, the bill's taken care of. Let's head back to Dumpsters."

They thanked Sonny for his generosity as they drove back. Bob pulled in front; they got out of the Jeep and went in. It was a sight to behold as they strutted down the hall in their uniforms. Every head turned—staff, residents, and visitors—they couldn't believe their eyes. They stopped to be acknowledged by Ms. Turnbuckle and the administrator. Mamie and Sally, giggling like a couple of schoolgirls, ran over to greet their heroes. Sonny and Bob stood by, joyfully savoring the significance of the moment.

Mamie said, "Fellows, Sally and I are so proud of both of you."

Sally asked, "By the way, where's the fish?"

"It's a long story," said Herman. "I'll explain later."

Louie's eyes filled, as he walked over to Sonny, saying, "Herman and I are both very happy, thanks to you and Bob." As he hugged them both, he said, "We will remember what you did for a couple of old codgers 'til the day we die."

"You're welcome," Sonny said. "All the gratitude Bob and I needed was to see the expression on your faces as everyone came over to congratulate you."

After agreeing they would soon visit the camp, Sonny and Bob headed for the door. Sonny turned and said, "Don't forget your good deed."

The following day, Sonny's phone rang. It was Louie. "Hello Sonny, wait till you hear this. Mamie and Sally joined the Girls' Troop," he said. "They went over to the local council in Stroudsburg and signed up. Then they went to Dinklehoofers to buy uniforms. After lunch, they'll be in front of the building selling cookies. What do you think of that?" he asked.

"That's great. Tell Mamie to put me down for three boxes of the Mints; I love them." Sonny continued, "Remember, Uncle Louie you must do a good deed. By the way, I have a free day Thursday; I think we should run up to the camp to return your papers."

"Sounds good to me," said Louie, "I guess Bob won't be able to come with us?"

"That's right, he'll be at work. How's 10:30 a.m.?" Sonny asked.

"Sounds good, I'll let Herman know. We'll be waiting out front," Louie said.

Arriving exactly at 10:30 a.m., Sonny found the dynamic duo waiting, dressed in full regalia. They got into the car and headed for the camp; this time it would be an official visit. "By the way," said Sonny, "I spoke to Mr. Richie; he gave me the green light to fish as your guest."

During the drive, Sonny asked if they had performed their good deeds.

"I did," said Herman. "At breakfast, one of the grill cooks was out sick, so I filled in."

"But," said Louie, "his good deed turned out to be bad for the rest of us."

"What do you mean?" asked Sonny.

"He fried the damn eggs in vinegar instead of oil," said Louie. "Need I say more?"

Sonny asked, "Have you done your good deed yet?"

"Not yet," he answered.

It was approximately 11:30 a.m. when they reached their destination. They parked the car and went into the headmaster's office. Mr. Richie was very receptive toward the new recruits.

"Hello, men," he said, "welcome to Camp Arrowhead. I'll take your papers."

Sonny handed him their completed forms. After inspection, he asked them to raise their hands and repeat the oath after him. Upon completion, Mr. Richie swore in the new recruits.

"By the way," said Mr. Richie, "if you're able to attend next Saturday, we're having our annual Snipe Hunt. Whoever catches the biggest one will be crowned Snipe King.

"Now that you're members of Troop 18, the facilities are at your disposal." They exchanged salutes, shook hands, and thanked the headmaster.

Mr. Richie said, "Now you can fish to your heart's content."

Sonny thanked Mr. Richie as they left the cabin and proceeded to Louie's fishing spot. After a short walk, they came to an opening. It was beautiful. A cool, silent stream meandered through the woodlands.

Louie said, "Follow the stream, it will lead us right to the lake." As they walked further down the trail, he said, "There it is."

Once they set down their gear, they picked out their poles and chose their spots. As they began to hook bait, Herman said, "While growing up in Scotland, my father took me fishing. One day he explained, 'I want you to learn how to fend for yourself. Remember this proverb: Give a man a fish; you feed him for a day. Give him a *can opener*, you feed him for life.'"

"Herman, that's the best fish story I ever heard," Sonny said. He was first to cast off, followed by the boys, whose lines became tangled as soon as they hit the water. Before a controversy ensued, Sonny laid down his pole and disentangled their lines, suggesting it would be better if they cast off in opposite directions. His suggestion panned out. A half hour passed without the least inkling of a bite. Worried their interest might wane, Sonny quietly went back to the car. From a bucket, he removed two live trout he purchased at the fish store earlier. He placed them into a pail and hurried back, to find the two old-timers sound asleep. Being quiet as a mouse, he pulled in their lines, positioning the store-bought fish onto their hooks. Then he threw them back into the water. Once the fish hit the surface, their lines began to tug. Sonny yelled over to wake them up.

They awakened simultaneously, shouting, "I got a hit, I got a hit!"

Sonny immediately yelled, "Quick, reel them in, but do it slowly or they'll get away." Following his directions, they did exactly as he suggested.

Louie reeled his catch in first. "Hot diggity," he shouted, "look at the size of this boy!"

As Herman attempted to reel in his catch, his line became lodged under a rock.

"Hold on a minute, Herman," Sonny said, "I'll free it."

Before Sonny could free his line, Herman's footing gave way. In he went, *kerplunk.* As he hit the water, he shouted, "I can't swim!"

Sonny rushed over, picked up the extra large net and was able to scoop him out. Once on land, Sonny helped him up, gave him a towel and asked how he felt.

He answered, "Like a wet fish out of water. Thanks, it would have been a shame to have lost my fish, especially since it's bigger than Louie's."

That did it. From that moment 'til they arrived at Dumpsters, they were continuously at each other's throats. Sonny just listened and laughed silently.

Once out of the car, Louie said, "Herman, this is a good opportunity for me to do my good deed. Hand me that miserable little sardine, and I'll give you this monster in exchange."

With that remark, they began where they left off. Sonny said good-bye, but it fell on deaf ears. He could still hear them carrying on as he approached the exit gate. Sonny couldn't wait to tell Bob what had happened, especially since he's a fisherman, who—like many others—loves a good fish story.

Chapter 6
Married to the Devil's Daughter

Another Wednesday rolled around, signaling that the time had arrived for Sonny to visit Louie. Before departing, he spoke to Bob, explaining the events that took place at Camp Arrowhead on Thursday. Bob was eager to learn of their experience and asked Sonny to give Louie and Herman his regards. "I certainly will, Bob," he said. "I'll be leaving to visit Uncle Louie as soon as I get off the phone." Once their conversation ended, Sonny made ready to drive to Dumpsters.

When he arrived, he ran into Herman. "Hello, Sonny," he said. "If you're looking for Louie, he just made a bee line for the john. He has a case of the G.I.'s."

"Was it something he ate?" asked Sonny.

"Yeah, he ate stewed prunes!" said Herman. "He had the runs all morning."

"By the way, Herman, Bob sends his regards. Do you mind if I wait with you?"

"I'd be delighted to sit and talk with you, Sonny. Your uncle thinks the world of you and says he's lucky to have you for a nephew."

"The feeling's mutual, Herman. I look forward to our meetings," Sonny said. "Here he comes now. Hi, Uncle Louie, how are you feeling?"

Drained, he answered, "I'll never eat prunes again, stewed or sober."

"Sit down," said Herman. "I'm on my way to play bingo with Sally in the recreation room. See you later."

As Herman got up, Louie sat beside Sonny. "How are you doing, my boy?" he asked.

"Not bad," Sonny said.

"Do I detect a hint of disenchantment?" Louie asked.

"Why do you ask?" Sonny said. "Is it that obvious?"

"It sure is," Louie answered. "I've worn that same look many times during my marriage to Carmela," he said. "Want to tell your old uncle about it? Sometimes it pays to get things off your chest."

Given the opportunity, Sonny unloaded. When he was finished telling Louie his mother-in-law was trying to destroy his marriage, he wondered if he had any advice to offer.

Louie gave him an earful. Without blinking an eye he said, "Sonny, don't think you're alone; we're all in the same boat. For instance, take my mother-in-law. When my father-in-law passed away, she decided to live with us. Feeling sorry she was alone, not wishing to have a confrontation with Carmela, I fell into the proverbial trap. From that moment on, my life became a nightmare. In she moved, bag and baggage. On the first day, Carmela said, 'Mama will have to sleep with me tonight 'til we get a new mattress; you can sleep in the guest room. You don't mind, do you?' What choice did I have? They both ganged up on me. 'All right,' I said. My mother-in-law frightened the hell out of me. She had a face that looked like 20 miles of bad road. As each day passed, I realized the old broad had to be Satan's wife. She tried everything in her satanical bag of tricks to destroy our fragile marriage. Living with them was a horror. The least little thing would set them off, and they'd chase me around the house."

"I can't believe it," said Sonny. "What did you do?"

"I ran into the closet and locked the door," he said. "The two of them would bang on the door screaming, 'Come out, you lily-livered yellow-belly.' They tried to goad me into opening the door."

"Did you?" Sonny asked.

"Hell no. In my house, I was the boss," Louie said.

"Each passing day, the situation became more explosive. The climax came one evening, after meeting some of the guys at the Italian Social Club. We played several games of bocce and had a few beers. Trying to drown my sorrows, I had one too many. It was after midnight by the time my buddy drove me home.

"I got out of the car and staggered into the house. I stripped off my clothing and tiptoed upstairs to the bedroom. As I slid between the sheets, I felt a chill coming on. Shivering, I snuggled close to Carmela. She felt warm as toast.

"Early the following morning, I had a strange feeling someone was standing over me. I opened my eyes, and after a few seconds they came into focus. There stood Carmela. In her hand, she held a cast iron frying pan. Squeamishly, I said, 'Hi Carmela.' 'Don't hi me,' she said. 'What's the big idea, you no-good drunken bum?' 'I don't understand what you mean.

What's wrong now?' I asked. 'You get out of that bed this minute. I'll show you what's wrong!' She yelled. 'What did I do? I know I may have had one too many last night, but is that any reason to go ballistic?' I asked. That's when the roof fell in, Sonny. 'You drunken idiot. Last night you went into the wrong bedroom. You slept with my mother,' she answered. 'That's impossible,' I said as I turned to look.

"Under the covers I noticed an obvious lump. Slowly I pulled them back exposing my mother-in-law. The sight of her sent me into partial shock. There she was stark naked, sporting a devilish grin that stretched across her face from ear to ear. Realizing what happened, I rushed into the bathroom to puke my guts out, wishing I were dead. You can bet, after that demeaning incident, I watched every move I made. Every time we sat down to eat, whenever I looked across the table, the old witch had that awful grin on her face.

"Then one day it hit me. I said, 'Mama, you know how you always say you're dying to visit your native Italy?' 'Yes Luigi,' she said, 'more than anything else.' 'Carmela,' I said, 'wouldn't it be wonderful if we paid to send mama to visit her family?' 'Yes,' she said, 'but we couldn't afford it.' 'Oh yes we can,' I said. 'I managed to save $3,000. I was going to surprise you. I know how much you love your mama. Let's do it.' 'How wonderful,' she said.

"Without another word, I picked up the phone and booked a one-way passage to Italy. In the interim, they both were sweet as pie. The days passed rapidly. On the day of departure, we drove to New York Harbor and saw her safely onboard. Once the ship steamed from the dock, I crossed myself as we both waved and threw kisses. After the liner faded from view, we got into our car and drove back. I must say, without Satan's wife around, our house was once again a home."

"By the way, how was her trip to Italy?" asked Sonny.

"I don't know," said Louie. "She never told us."

"Never told you?" asked Sonny. "I don't understand, didn't you ask?"

"No. Let me explain," replied Louie. "About three weeks passed when we received a long-distance call from Italy. The funeral director from La Casa de Morta (the house of death) called to notify me that the old witch had died. He said, 'Your mother-in-law suddenly passed away.' I asked what the cause of death was. He said, 'She was talking while eating a biscotti and choked.' Then he asked how he should dispose of the remains. At first

I thought a trash bag would be the cheapest way out. I asked, 'What are my options?' He said, 'Cemetery plot, mausoleum, or crematorium, which do you prefer?'"

"What did you tell him, Uncle Louie?" asked Sonny.

I said, "*Take no chances, do all three!*"

"Uncle Louie, are you pulling my leg?" Sonny asked.

"Well, maybe a bit, but there's a moral to the story," he said.

"What might that be?" Sonny asked.

"Keep focused," he said, "in the event your mother-in-law mentions her desire to visit somewhere, especially if she says, 'I'm dying to go.' Do everything possible to grant her wish, even if it means footing the bill. I hope I've been of some help."

"To be honest," Sonny said, "what you've told me has my wheels spinning."

"Good," answered Louie. "Would you like to continue our discussion about the good old days, Sonny?"

"Yes," he said. "Please begin with the time you were a youngster and helped grandpa in the store."

"Sure. Now let me see. I really got into the flow of things around my twelfth birthday. My weekday began around 6:00 a.m. Except for Mondays and Thursdays; those were the days Papa went down to the fresh produce market on Mulberry Street in Newark, New Jersey. I'd awaken at 4:00 a.m., allowing myself ample time to get up and dress. As I did, I was able to smell the freshly-brewed coffee. Papa buttered kaiser rolls and toasted them on pie tins. Dunked in a cup of java made them a special treat I'll never forget. After breakfast, we left for the market.

"All the vendors liked Papa. They nicknamed him *Bullets*. In fact, that's the name they wrote on the invoices. While Papa shopped for produce, I got to taste all the fresh fruits. Back in those days, we bought only fruits that tasted good, so the customers always got the best. Unlike today, when you shop at the supermarket and buy fruit, they always seem tasteless. You see, Sonny, years ago, they were picked after they had ripened on the tree. Do you realize today, bananas and most tomatoes are gassed in order to ripen them?

"Another thing—in the old days, meats bought daily at the slaughterhouse were delivered directly to our store. My father would hang them on metal hooks in a holding cooler to age. The aging process allowed the meat to tenderize. When you cut into the steak and took your first bite, you thought you died and went to heaven. When Papa bought imported provolone, he would not slice it 'til it aged."

"How did he do that?" Sonny asked.

"Down in the cellar, where it was cool, he'd hang these six-foot long cheeses by thin ropes. He'd remove a plug from the cheese to taste it. He would slice them only when ripe."

"Didn't they dry out?" Sonny asked.

"Not at all," Louie answered. "He'd wrap the provolone with cheese cloth. Every two weeks during the process, he would rub the outside with good imported Italian olive oil. As the cheese aged, it shrank, and as it shrank, it would draw in the oil to bathe it. Of course the shrinkage was costly. But taste and texture were incomparable. He sold the cheese for a mere 85 cents per pound. Nowadays, that provolone sells for 11 to 12 dollars a pound and tastes like soap.

"Using the very best pork and spices, Grandpa made the best Italian sausage money could buy. I remember working alongside him, filling customers' orders 'til one or two o'clock in the morning. People flocked from all over to get Papa's Italian *salsiccia*. When Papa became ill, his doctor advised him to sell the business and retire. Before he closed the store, he gave his time-tested recipe to the new owners. Using Papa's formula, they began making his now-famous sausage. Many of his former customers would stop by to visit him. They'd remark that new owner's sausage was not as good as when Papa made it."

"Why not, if they followed his recipe?" Sonny asked.

"The only thing I could think of is while mixing the ingredients, as he leaned over the container, accidentally *ashes from his Italian stogie* dropped into the mix. That's the secret ingredient they left out!"

Smiling, Sonny said, "Gosh, Uncle Louie. I don't know if you're kidding, but that's a funny story." As he gazed at his watch, he said, "Holy mackerel! It's nearly 4:00 p.m. I promised Jo I'd take her shopping. I must run. I'll be back next week. Bye, Uncle Louie."

"Good-bye, Sonny. Remember, when you shop for Italian sausage, make sure the list of ingredients includes ashes from an Italian stogie, or it won't taste as good as Grandpa's."

When Sonny arrived home, Jo was patiently waiting. She got into the car and they drove to the supermarket. Sonny parked the car, picked up a shopping cart and entered the store. Jo enjoyed shopping there because of the wide selection of quality products they carried at reasonable prices.

While Jo shopped, Sonny decided to park himself on a bench adjacent to the checkout counters. He got a kick out of watching the mix of characters going through the lines. It was every bit as entertaining as sitting on a bench at the seashore or mall.

At last, Jo arrived with her basket of goodies. While the clerk checked the items on the register, Sonny packed. He preferred packing his own bags; that way he could separate the items according to categories, which made unpacking much easier. During the process, he began snickering. Upon completion, they left the store, put the bags in the trunk, and then drove away.

Once on the road, Jo asked, "Now do you want to tell me what's so funny?"

"What do you mean?" Sonny asked.

"At the checkout counter, I caught you laughing. What was that about?"

"Oh that," Sonny answered. "You're not going to believe this, but here goes. While I waited for you to check out, I sat watching other shoppers go through the lines. It was extremely entertaining, especially when an elderly couple, well into their eighties, checked out. First, the clerk rang up the items. Then the elderly woman opened a large tote bag, pulling from it what seemed like hundreds of coupons. The total receipt registered $98.00. This meant the poor clerk had to reenter the entire list once again. Only this time he had to deduct the coupon discounts. In the meantime, the line was growing. Watching their facial expressions was a show in itself. Seeing the backup, the store manager called for two additional clerks to man the registers.

"Finally the clerk handed the woman her receipt. Using the corresponding coupons, he told her the total bill had been reduced to $63.00. That's when all hell broke loose. The old gent with her was beside himself. He refused to pay the bill, creating a commotion. Everyone in the other aisles began rubbernecking, trying to determine the cause of the disturbance. It was reminiscent of a traffic jam on Route 80. With a smile on his face, the store manager walked over and entered the fray. He introduced himself to the elderly couple. All eyes watched as he asked, 'What seems to be the problem? May I be of assistance?'

"By now the elderly man, who worked himself into a dither, began shouting. 'Please sir, try to calm yourself,' said the manager. 'I'm sure this can be worked out.'

On that note, the elderly man settled down. The manager turned to the clerk. 'What's the problem?'

"The clerk responded, 'Well Mr. Nicely, I followed procedure, deducting the discount coupons from the total bill, which left a balance of $63.00. This gentleman refuses to pay.'

"Turning to the old gent, the manager said, 'According to the clerk, that's the balance, less discounts.'

"Fuming, the elderly man said, 'Wait a minute! What about the rest of these coupons?' There were literally hundreds of them. 'I'm sorry sir, but I'm only able to credit one coupon per item,' answered the manager.

"The crowd waited for the old gent's reaction. They didn't have long to wait.

"The old man became belligerent. 'I demand you honor these coupons. My dear wife has been collecting them for a year. We're not budging 'til we get satisfaction.'

"The crowd loved the underdog, even though in their hearts they knew he was wrong. They started clapping and hissing at the beleaguered manager. Seeing no way out, under extreme pressure, he advised the clerk to honor all coupons."

"You've got to be kidding," said Jo.

"No I'm not. In the final outcome, the couple not only got the entire grocery order free, but were paid an additional $36.50 for the remaining coupons. In the end, the watchful crowd roared in approval.

"Now for the clincher. The old gent shook the manager's hand, thanking him, saying, 'I can see you're a smart businessman. As soon as my wife collects another batch of coupons, we'll be back.'"

"What happened then?" Jo asked.

"Well" said Sonny "As the couple prepared to exit the store, the elderly woman noticing someone lying on the floor said, 'Oh my, what happened?' A gentleman answered, 'It seems the manager fainted.' In response she said, 'Poor soul, he must have high blood pressure.'"

With that, unable to hold back, both Jo and Sonny burst out laughing, continuing to do so in spurts until they arrived home.

Chapter 7
A Brief Medical History

Sonny dropped by to visit Louie. Entering Dumpsters, he was surprised to find the absence of the usual hustle and bustle he'd come to expect. Looking about, he noticed there was no one in sight. He thought, "Where could everyone be?" Coming from the direction of the recreation room, he heard the faint sound of music. Deciding to further investigate, Sonny moseyed down the corridor. Drawing closer, the music intensified. When he reached the source, he spied through the window. To his surprise, he saw the residents and staff listening to a musical presentation. He caught Ms. Turnbuckle's eye. Acknowledging his presence, she invited him in. Whispering in his ear, she explained that a choral group from a nearby church stopped over to entertain the residents. She told him he had arrived in time to join the sing-along. Louie turned, noticing Sonny. He waved for him to come forward. Spotting an empty seat, he tiptoed to it and sat down. Happy to see him, the gang smiled.

The first song performed was the old favorite "Carolina in the Morning." Everyone was encouraged to join in, and that's exactly what they did. Each song that followed put them in the mood to continue singing. It was a wonderful celebration of spirit and song. At the program's conclusion, the recreation room emptied as residents made their way back to their respective floors. Louie and Sonny opted to sit on the veranda. The large, airy, screened-in porch offered a pleasant respite. Early-1900-type rockers added to the cozy atmosphere.

An aide assigned to the area asked if they cared for a beverage. Unfamiliar with the drink menu, Sonny asked for a cold beer. Louie laughed, saying "Sorry, Sonny, the strongest beverage available in this establishment is a Shirley Temple." Embarrassed, Sonny asked for iced tea instead.

"Millie, you can double that order," said Louie.

As they rocked in the chairs sipping their drinks, Sonny said, "What a gorgeous day."

"Yes" said Louie, "Reminds me of Florida in April."

"Did you spend much time in Florida?"

"Sure did. When I was married to Carmela, we wintered there. The natives referred to us as snowbirds. Our condo was located in a 55-or-older senior development called Pine Ridge IV, located in the city of Greenacres." As he spoke, Louie thought of those bygone days. Tears ran down the side of his face. "It was a wonderful place, Sonny. Everyone was friendly and cared for one another. The owners were mainly from New Jersey, Massachusetts, and New York. Like other seniors living in the community, we had our share of medical problems.

"Carmela developed chest pains. I took her to see a cardiologist. He was an excellent practitioner, but had a terrible bedside manner. After numerous tests, she was diagnosed with two blocked arteries. The surgeon performed double-bypass surgery. The procedure was done by a team of very competent specialists at J.F.K. Hospital in Atlantis, Florida. The care she received, both pre-and post-op, couldn't have been better. After her discharge, she returned home to our condo, weakened and fragile from the ordeal. She was warned to take it easy for at least a month. Luckily for both of us, I happen to be a good housekeeper, cook, and baker as well."

"Most men can't boil water, probably because they've never tried," said Sonny.

"That's true," said Louie. "Let me tell you, women have it tough. Their day never ends. Living in a condo community, everyone knows everyone else's business. It's difficult to keep a secret. Neighbors dropped in to visit Carmela while she was recuperating. Carmela surprised me by telling them how wonderful I was. She bragged of my many talents. I couldn't believe my ears. In the past, she never gave me credit for anything! Once word got around the community, it spread like wildfire. Everyone found out. In no time, I received dozens of proposals. I recall one in particular. It read, 'In the event Carmela doesn't make it, I'm available.'"

"Boy, Uncle Louie, those old ladies didn't waste any time, did they?"

"Ladies?" said Louie. "The proposals I refer to were from men!"

"You old codger, got me again, didn't you?" said Sonny.

"Yes my boy, guess I did. It's a given, in life nobody gets a free ride. Sooner or later, the wheel of misfortune stops. When your number's up, there's not a damn thing you can do. That's life. We never know what's in the cards. We must learn to accept the hand we're dealt. No matter how hard the row to hoe gets, never throw in the towel, above all, 'never say uncle!'

"I know from personal experience. A urologist misdiagnosed me for prostate cancer. He failed to do proper testing, even though I suggested he do further tests. Through my own perseverance and personal research, I was able to find the facts. Never accept any one doctor's diagnosis. Get second and third opinions, especially when your life's at stake. After all, he's only some guy on the end of a finger. It's your ass that's on the line!"

"What type of treatments were you given?"

"At the time, I was only in my mid-sixties. Before surgery, I was given a course of female hormones."

"What was that like?" asked Sonny.

"It was living hell. From the hormone injections, I developed all sorts of problems."

"What do you mean?"

"First, my belly went soft, similar to a woman's after childbirth. Then I had never-ending bouts of hot flashes. That's when I discovered what women go through during menopause. It was awful. Soon after, my tits began sprouting. Then I had to wear a training bra. I managed to adjust to everything. That is..."

"That is, what?" asked Sonny.

"Well, I'm a little embarrassed to talk about it. I guess I can tell you. When I got dressed in the morning, I had trouble deciding whether to put on my underwear or Carmela's."

"Uncle Louie, try to be serious. How did the surgery go?"

"Not bad," said Louie. "After a short hospital stay, I came home. Now it was Carmela's turn to nurture me back to health. Because of my weakened condition, Medicare provided home care. Arrangements were made through the hospital for an aide to come bathe me. I'll never forget the day the doorbell rang. Carmela opened the door to find a beautiful young lady standing there.

"'I'm from the Visiting Aides' Association,' she said. 'I'm here to bathe Mr. Fettuccine.' Uninvitingly, Carmela said, 'He's in there!' Somewhat skeptical, she came in and introduced herself. 'I'm Miss Cleanwhistle,' she said. 'I'm here to bathe you, Mr. Fettuccine. Where's the bathroom?' Swinging open the door, Carmela said, 'Right here.'

"Miss Cleanwhistle helped me into the bathroom, where I sat on the closed toilet seat. As she prepared, I reached over to shut the door. Knowing Carmela to be extremely jealous, I was not surprised to see the door creak back open. In the mirror, I could see Carmela's reflection standing just outside. While the young lady helped me strip down, I watched Carmela's changing facial expressions.

"'Nice and easy, Mr. Fettuccine,' said the young lady. 'I'll help you into the shower.' While doing so, she told me she had recently been discharged from the service. 'I also was in the service,' I said.

"After regulating the shower, she proceeded to lather me up. She rinsed me off and said, 'Mr. Fettuccine sir, you will have to wash your private.' With that, the bathroom door flung completely open. Hands on hips, quite indignant stood Carmela. Turning in response to the door opening, Miss Cleanwhistle looked in astonishment.

"Carmela immediately lashed out at the young lady. 'Miss Clogwhistle, or whatever your name is, do not refer to *It* as private! *It* may be standing down now, but I'll have you know, in *Its* heyday what you're looking at was a *private,* first class. Show *It* some respect. It may be difficult to believe, but *It* had its share of hard times during *Its* long, illustrious career. I agree, *It's* just an old softee now, but when aroused, *It* always rose to the occasion. If you can't handle *It,* let me know.' Turning to walk out, Carmela said, 'Young lady, remember, in the words of the great General Douglas MacArthur, *Old soldiers never die, they just fade away,*' as she walked out, slamming the door.

"Unable to assimilate the gist of what happened, Miss Cleanwhistle stood with her jaw hanging."

"How about you, Uncle Louie?" asked Sonny. "What were you doing?"

"Me?" said Louie. "I was left holding my own!"

"Wow," said Sonny. "Aunt Carmela placed you in a compromising position. Incidentally, were you in much pain post-surgery?"

"No, not at all. Although I did notice one change, whenever we had sex it was hard for me to tell whether I was coming or going. After that experience, I made sure I kept close watch on my medical history."

"While we're on the subject, did either of you have any other problems?" asked Sonny.

"Yes," said Louie. "Years ago, I had trouble breathing. Insisting I see a doctor, Carmela made an appointment with her cardiologist. Arriving at his office, Carmela sat as I approached the receptionist. Sealed behind a sliding glass window, she completely ignored me while continuing to type. In the meantime, I entered my name and the time of day onto a pad. Patiently, I waited to be noticed. Finally, the glass window slid open. She looked, without cracking a smile, and said, 'Yes?' Befuddled by her sudden expression of heartfelt emotion, I said, 'I'm Louie Fettuccine. I'm here for my 8:00 a.m. appointment.' Excitement hit fever pitch when she said, 'What insurance do you have?' I removed the cards from my wallet. 'Let me have them,' she growled. In exchange, she handed me a clipboard, containing three pages with writing on both sides. 'Take a seat and fill them out.' She reminded me of my drill sergeant with P.M.S.

"I never took time to learn my Florida address or phone number, so I turned to Carmela for help. Embarrassed as everyone listened, I said, 'Carmela, where do we live?' Writing it down, I asked, 'What's our phone number?' As I began filling out the insurance portion, I thought to myself, 'I gave her my insurance cards to copy; I'll be damned if I'm going to fill this out.' Turning to the medical history, I was bewildered by many of the questions, especially those pertaining to surgery. I wondered what purpose would be served if I listed a hemorrhoidectomy. I didn't want to make it too easy for him. I thought, 'That's what he's getting paid for. Let him figure out what the hell's wrong with me!'

"Deciding to leave the sheet blank, I walked up to the window to find someone else sitting there. The window slid back and she asked, 'Do you have an appointment?' 'Yes,' I answered, 'my appointment was at 8:00 a.m.' Looking at the clock, which now read 11:00 a.m., she turned to me very much miffed and said, 'You're late! Who is your insurance carrier?' 'When I got here three hours ago it was Medicare. But you know Congress, by now they may have decided to cut funding.' 'Humph,' she said, as she began closing the sliding window. Stopping it with my hand, I said, 'Would you be so kind as to explain the fine print?' She read, 'If your insurance company fails to pay this bill, you will be held responsible to fulfill your obligation.' 'How come you left out, under penalty of death?' I asked. Believe it or not, she smiled.

"I walked back, sat down and closed my eyes to wait. The office door opened, and out walked an individual asking for Mr. Fafaroni. No one responded. Again she asked, 'Is Luigi Fafaroni here?' I said, 'You wouldn't be looking for me, Mr. Fettuccine, would you?' 'Yes,' she said. 'Come in; you're late. The doctor has to leave for an emergency.' Taking a deep breath, I kept my composure and followed her.

"'I want to weigh you,' she said. 'Hop on the scale.' I thought to myself, 'If anyone should be getting weighed, it should be her,' she had an ass as big as a barn door. She said, 'Sorry about the name mix up. I should have known better, fettuccine is my favorite pasta.' My mind began playing tricks. I had a vision of myself sprawled across a plate as this behemoth of a woman sat down to partake of her fettuccine. Licking her chops, she tied a napkin across her bosom, preparing to eat her favorite pasta, as she sprinkled parmesan all over. I became quite anxious, wondering how much she could devour at one sitting. Then suddenly, as her fork moved in closer, I heard a voice calling, 'Fettuccine! Fettuccine, you're next.'

"Opening my eyes, I felt Carmela poking my ribs, telling me to wake up, the nurse was calling. Startled, I jumped from my chair, hurrying in the nurse's direction.

"As I entered the inner office, the nurse said, 'Step up on the scale.' It was déjà vu. After the weigh-in, I was shown to an examining room, where I was asked to strip down to my birthday suit, put on a Johnny coat, and wait. Twenty minutes passed when finally the door opened, and in walked another female.

"'I'm the nurse practitioner. Climb onto the table. I want to check your blood pressure and do an EKG.' I figured she must have been the opening act, and the doctor would be coming on stage any minute. Sure enough, as she left, he walked in. Offering a muffled hello, almost uninterested, he just about noticed my presence. Then he sat on a stool at a small desk. As he picked up the charts, the phone rang. After hanging up the receiver, he began grilling me, as he scribbled while I answered his questions. I noted he was making check marks on a form. The phone rang again. Answering, the tone of his voice changed to that of anger. Concluding his conversation, he slammed the receiver down, got up, and left the room.

"Left to sit and wait, I stretched over to peek at my chart. I was surprised to learn, that instead he had been looking over his stock report. I assumed the guy he was speaking with must have been his broker.

"When he returned, still upset, he said, 'I want to listen to your chest.' Placing his ice-cold stethoscope firmly against my pecs, he told me to breathe deeply. Next he said, 'Cough.' As I did, the inter-office buzzer sounded. Picking it up, he said, 'Seems like a lost cause to me.' You know how your mind plays games, don't you, Sonny?"

"I sure do," said Sonny.

"When the doctor said 'lost cause,' was he referring to me or his stock portfolio? 'I'm ordering a stress test,' he said. 'Another one?' I asked. 'What do you mean, another one?' he said. At that point, Sonny, I'd had enough. I let him have it.

"'What do I mean? I'll tell you what I mean! My appointment was for 8:00 a.m. I sat in your waiting room for three hours. I had to put up with your rude office help. Obviously, trained by you. You all have matching personalities. During my examination, you upset me. I thought you were looking at my chart, while all the time, it was your stock reports. Now you have the balls to order a stress test? What the hell do you think I've been under for the last three hours? I'm stressed plenty! Come now, Doc. Give me a break. Can't you at least tell me what you found so far?'

"At this point, he said, 'It seems as though you have a valve that's leaking.' I questioned, 'A leaking valve? You mean to say after all this time and aggravation, all you came up with is a slow leak?' 'Yes,' said the doctor. 'Why do you ask in that manner?' 'A year ago, my urologist made that same diagnosis.' Ignoring my pun, he said, 'Mr. Fettuccine, get this prescription filled. The drug will help regulate the blood flow through your valve. It should keep you from becoming short of breath.' 'Thanks,' I said. 'Maybe you'll go easy on the bill, so I don't get short of cash either.' Would you believe he actually laughed?

"He handed me my charts and told me to stop at the front desk. After doing so, I walked out into the waiting room, which by now was deserted with the exception of Carmela. We put on our coats and left."

"How were you after that?" asked Sonny.

"Several years later," said Louie, "I developed a rapid heartbeat. The cardiologist implanted a pacemaker. Before leaving the hospital, the doctor said, 'Fettuccine, if you develop a problem with your pacemaker, don't be upset. I can easily adjust the pacing over the phone.' In jest I said, 'I doubt that, Doc, my number's unlisted!' Too bad!"

Sonny said, "What do you mean?"

"Too bad. He was a good doctor. He committed suicide," said Louie. "The market did him in."

Chapter 8
Nightmares for Nincompoops

The next several days, Jo and Sonny spent time visiting with his sister and brother-in-law in New Jersey. They had tickets for a Mets/Red Sox game. Already late for the opening pitch, with traffic moving at a snail's pace, Sonny challenged his overly cautious brother-in-law to pass the line of cars in front. Stubbornly refusing, his brother-in-law blurted out, "Are you crazy? You wanna end up in the cemetery?" Unfortunately, they had no choice. The cars ahead happened to be the tail end of a funeral procession. Though they enjoyed their visit, it felt good to get home. They loved their home in the Poconos, mainly because their children and grandchildren lived close by.

After a good night's rest, the following morning Sonny took care of long overdue chores. When finished, he left for Dumpsters. As he entered the facility, he bumped into Ms. Turnbuckle. After exchanging greetings, she asked if he had a few minutes to spare.

While sitting in her office, she said, "Perhaps I'm making more of this than I should, but I was wondering, has your uncle mentioned his recurring nightmares?"

"No," Sonny said, "he hasn't."

"That's odd. I thought for sure you'd be the first he'd confide in."

"Yes, you're right. I wonder why he hasn't told me about them. What happened?"

"According to the nurse on the 11-7 shift, he continually dreams and wakes up screaming. It's been going on for the past couple of weeks. I thought, when you're alone, you might draw him out. Above all, please use discretion. I wouldn't want him to discover we had this conversation."

"You can count on me, Ms. Turnbuckle. I won't let him catch on," Sonny answered.

"Thank you, Sonny. I certainly appreciate it."

"No problem," he said as they shook hands.

After leaving her office, Sonny went directly to Louie's room. Entering the room, he found him sleeping soundly. Not wishing to awaken him, Sonny quietly sat in the lounge chair. Resting on a table immediately adjacent was a novel entitled *Nightmares for Nincompoops*. As Sonny fingered through the pages, he realized why his Uncle Louie was having such darn awful dreams. From what little he was able to read, he found the book to be quite scary.

Unconsciously, Louie rolled onto his back. His eyes opened slightly and caught a quick glimpse of Sonny. While focusing his half-closed eyes, he uttered in a muffled voice, as one does when first awakening, "Is that you, Sonny?" As he became more cognizant, he said, "I didn't hear you come in. Guess I dozed off."

"Hi, Uncle Louie. I was looking through your book. It's a little scary, isn't it?"

"It sure as hell is, Sonny." I picked it up from the bookmobile after Dr. Feelfine advised me to read a book at bedtime. He said it would help me fall asleep."

"Has it?" Sonny asked.

"Yes and no. I get to sleep all right, but then I have the screwiest dreams."

"Can you tell me about them?"

"Sure. A couple of weeks ago, I read the first chapter and fell off. I guess it was around two in the morning. I had a feeling someone was watching me. Suddenly, I jumped up in bed. A cold sweat came over me. 'Who's there?' I asked. 'Who's there?'

"A voice answered, 'Don't be frightened, Louie, it's only me.'

"'Who are you?' I asked, stuttering from fright. 'What do you want?'

"'I don't want anything, Louie. I'm the devil. I want to be your friend. I dropped by to see how you were.' His raspy voice sent a chill down my spine as I began shaking uncontrollably. Then I did something I haven't done since childhood."

"What's that?" asked Sonny.

"I peed the bed!" said Louie. "As the *beast* rose from the chair, it cast an eerie figure that moved ever closer. The moonlight coming through the window played upon it. There's no doubt whatsoever it was Lucifer. Coming from this monster was one of the most putrid odors imaginable. The only thing that comes close is morning diaper change on Unit #2."

"What happened next?" asked Sonny.

"Screaming at the top of his voice, the devil said, 'I'm extremely disappointed, Louie,' as flames spewed from his mouth. Floundering for the right words, I asked, 'What? What did I do?' 'I'll tell you,' said the devil. 'Nothing, you've done nothing wrong. You're too damn good!' he growled. 'How in the world do you ever expect to go to hell?' he shouted. 'If you continue to behave this way, I'll...I'll take away your bridgework.' 'I don't have any,' I said. Covering my head as I cowered, I felt warmth return to the room. My chills and fears vanished into thin air.

"Suddenly I heard a voice say, 'Do not be afraid, Louie, I'm with you.' Opening my eyes, I asked, 'Where are you? I can't see you.' 'You won't be able to. Nevertheless, I'm here, sitting in your chair.' 'Are you the Ghost of Christmas Past?' 'No, Louie' was the answer. 'How about Christmas Present?' Again the response was 'No.' 'Maybe you're Christmas Future?' 'No!' the voice said. 'You're not even warm.' 'Warm,' I said. 'I know you're the devil in disguise. You're playing with me, aren't you?'

"'Ho ho, relax Louie,' the voice said. 'I'll give you a hint. My initials are H.G.' 'H.G.! Holy moly! That's it. Now I know; you're...you're the Holy Ghost.' 'That's right, Louie. That's who I am. But you can call me H.G.' I asked, 'H.G., how come they gave you the boot?' 'I haven't the slightest inkling,' said H.G. Then I said, 'Perhaps the Big Guy felt you needed a rest? In any case, it took Catholics a long time to get used to the change.' 'That's my only regret,' said H.G.

"'Do you mind if I ask something personal?' 'No, not at all, Louie. Go right ahead,' was his answer. 'Were you given a golden parachute?' 'No,' was the reply. 'That's a shame,' I said. 'I hope they at least gave you Social Security and Medicare benefits.' 'I'm afraid not,' he said.

"I then asked, 'Do you still play the horn?' 'It's been quite awhile, back since the time of Gabriel. But my lip is still strong,' he said. 'Good, my nephew Sonny's grandson, Mark, is friendly with a ghost named Gasper. He's playing a gig on Halloween. Maybe you can sit in.' 'I don't think so, Louie, but thanks for asking.'

"'By the way, H.G.,' I said, 'whatever happened to Christopher? Not only was he a saint, but a silver medalist to boot! How come they gave him his walking papers?' 'Actually, he already had them,' said H.G. 'You know, H.G., it's a little scary to think that could happen,' I said. 'I guess the powers that be had their reasons,' said H.G. I told him, 'Things are not the same since Chris got canned. Traffic's increased. There are airline delays, lost luggage, tight seating, and higher ticket prices. All have added to the traveler's dilemma. The air traffic controllers are up in the air. At times, they don't know whether they're coming or going. We sure miss Chris.' H.G. said, 'I'm sorry, Louie, but I have to run. I hope I haven't spooked you.'"

"My gosh," said Sonny, "that was one heck of a dream. You know something? I'll bet you can write your own book."

"Wait, there's more," Louie said. "I asked H.G. if he was enjoying retirement."

"What did he say?" asked Sonny.

"H.G. said he missed the gang, but enjoyed the benefits of being able to sleep late. Then he asked, 'What did the Prince of Darkness want?' I said, 'He wanted to know if I attended Mass.' 'What did you tell him?' asked H.G. 'I told him Absolutely! I told him I belonged to the K. of C. and played bingo religiously,' I said.

"H.G. then asked 'Is there anything you're not telling me, Louie?' At that point, I didn't want H.G. to think I was lying."

"What did you tell him?" asked Sonny.

"I explained to him exactly what I told the devil. I said, 'Mr. Devil, sir, I'm really on your side.' Of course I said to H.G., 'You know I was only kidding!'"

"How did H.G. respond to that?" asked Sonny.

"He said, 'It's a known fact, whenever someone's back is against the wall, they always look for the easy way out.' Then he said, 'Isn't that right, Louie?'"

"How true," said Sonny. "Did he have anything else to say?"

"Yes, he told me he ran into Carmela and her mother. He said, Carmela asked how soon it would be before I joined her. He asked if I had a message I wanted him to deliver to her."

"Did you give him one?" asked Sonny.

"Yes, I said, 'Tell Carmela her old man stopped by tonight. He told me to tell her to go to hell! *He misses her.*' With that, H.G. said, 'Ta ta, Louie', I must run. I have to catch the soul train. If you need me, just call my name.'"

"That dream is truly amazing. Are there any others you can tell me about?" asked Sonny.

"Yes, but first I have to shed a tear."

While waiting Sonny picked up the book, continuing where he left off. After ten minutes or so, Louie came out dressed in street clothes.

"When you get older, it takes forever to get going. There are so many things to remember."

"Like what?" said Sonny.

"Like pulling up my zipper. Even more important," said Louie, "pulling it down. Now let's see, you want to hear about another dream." Louie thought for a moment, "Oh yes, here's a good one."

"If it's half as good as the last one, it'll be a real piperoo," Sonny said.

"In February, while you and Jo were down south, we had one heck of a blizzard," Louie said.

"Yes, I remember reading about it in the papers," said Sonny.

"During that period, Dumpsters experienced a nursing shortage. At one point, with the exception of Ms. Turnbuckle and her assistant, you couldn't find a nurse for hide nor hair. To complicate matters, Monroe County was in the midst of the worst flu epidemic to hit the area."

"My" said Sonny, "sounds as if things couldn't get any worse."

"That's exactly what I thought," said Louie. "Hear me out. Just as we entered a new week, we were battered by an additional foot of snow. Traffic along the East Coast remained bottled up. Ms. Turnbuckle, her assistant, and what few aides were left became ill or were snowbound. Residents were dropping like flies. The situation was horrendous."

"Gosh, Uncle Louie, what did you do?"

"Those of us left standing pitched in, doing whatever we could to help. Attempts to reach us from outside the community were in vain. One evening, exhausted, I went to my room, dropped on my bed, and fell asleep. I guess it was about 3 a.m. when I was suddenly awakened by the cries for help from other residents. Struggling to get to my feet, my knees buckled. I became light-headed as the room began to spin. I wiped the perspiration from my brow. I was burning up. Finally I realized my turn had come. Wringing wet, incoherent, my vision blurred, I attempted to make it into the hallway."

"Then what?" asked Sonny.

"I passed out, but not for long. At least that was my recollection. When I came to, I opened my eyes. Hovering over me were two women from housekeeping. Weak, unable to utter a sound, I could only watch and listen to their conversation. One of the women directed her subordinate to fetch a large bucket of ice water. When she returned, she placed it by my side. Figuring they were preparing to bring down my fever by giving me an ice bath, I smiled and waited. To my surprise the woman in charge dunked her floor mop into the ice water and began swabbing me down, as if I were the deck of an old battleship. Delirious from shock, I passed out a second time!"

"For how long?" asked Sonny.

"That's hard to say. If I had to venture a guess, I'd say 20 minutes. When I finally came to, the pungent smell of cabbage boiling filled my nostrils. Chilled, butt naked, I found myself face down across a butcher block. Looking around, still in a stupor, I slowly raised my head. Off at the far end of the room, standing in the corner, I faintly made out two figures dressed in white. Suspecting they were physicians brought in to attend the ailing, I relaxed. I heard one of them speaking on the phone, most likely reporting his progress. As he hung up, a third very large figure joined them. As they walked in my direction, I was able to determine who they were. Realization set in. I put two and two together. It was the chef and two of his cooks. 'But why?' I asked. 'What are they up to?'

"Still slightly incoherent, I said, 'What in hell am I doing lying butt naked on a butcher block? What's happening?' The large man said, 'It's me, Big Sam, the chef. Don't you recognize me?' 'Sure I do. Thank goodness it's you. Sam, tell me, why I'm here in the kitchen?' I asked him. 'Because of the nursing shortage, Dr. Feelfine called, asking those of us remaining to help out. Except for the two ladies from housekeeping and us, no one has been able to make it in. My staff and I have been here for the past three days,' he said. 'I know the ladies you speak of,' I said. 'They stripped me down and swabbed the deck.'

"'What are you guys up to?' I asked. 'Us?' said Sam. 'We were told to take temperatures.' 'Oh, I see,' I said. 'Wait 'til I roll over?' 'No,' he answered. 'Just open wide!' As I opened my mouth, he said, 'No Louie. Wrong end.' 'Oh,' I said. 'You're taking it through the bung hole!' Smiling, Sam yelled, 'Hey James, bring over that can of lard!' 'Lard?! What the hell do you need lard for?' I asked. 'Oh,' said Sam, 'that's so I can slide it in without hurting.' 'Slide it in? Slide what in? What do you think my ass is? A pork butt?' I yelled. 'Well, Louie, now that you mention it, would you rather have bone in or out? What do you think, James?' Sam said turning to his assistant. 'Sure enough, 'cept Louie's butt is sagging a bit,' was his answer. I said, 'Come on fellas. Can I help it if my skin doesn't fit anymore? By the way, what kind of thermometer is that you're holding?' 'A *meat* thermometer,' answered Sam. Smiling, he turned. In his hand, he was holding something that looked to be about 12 inches long. He began rubbing it with the lard. Next thing I knew, he called to his two helpers. 'OK boys, I got it pretty well greased. Spread 'em wide!'"

"You poor man; that must have been horrible," said Sonny. "What was the outcome?"

"I blacked out again. Next thing I heard was a voice saying, 'Louie, Louie, wake up. I took your rectal temperature. Your fever has broken. You're going to be just fine.' I looked up to see Ms. Turnbuckle. 'You haven't eaten in four days,' she said. 'Sam cooked some delicious pork butt and cabbage. Would you like some?' 'Yes,' I said. 'I would. Tell Sam, as long as it isn't mine. I'm sure he'll understand.' On that note, I rolled over and fell back to sleep."

"Am I to understand the entire story, including the flu epidemic, was a nightmare?" asked Sonny.

"Yes, Sonny, it was. I've saved the scariest dream for last. Before I tell you about it, let's get a cup of coffee. Follow me over to the coffee klatch. It's something new they've added for residents and families to enjoy."

As they entered, lo and behold, the first person they ran into was Big Sam. "Hi gentlemen," he said.

"Hello Sam, how's it going?" asked Louie. "You look a little upset. Something wrong?"

"I burned my pork butt," said Sam.

"How come?" asked Louie.

"I've misplaced my meat thermometer."

Uncle Louie and Sonny exchanged glances, turned laughing under their breath, and walked over to sit and drink their coffee.

"Now Sonny, let me tell you about my most recent nightmare," said Louie. "It was a crazy dream about winning a trip to Australia."

"What!" said Sonny, "How did that come about?"

"Several days ago when Ms. Turnbuckle handed me a brown envelope, sent by one of those pesky clearinghouses. The notice said, you could be the winner if you have the matching numbers."

"Come now, Uncle Louie, everybody receives those contest forms in the mail," said Sonny. "Did you honestly believe you were going to win?"

"At first I felt as you do," said Louie. "That was until last evening. I began thinking about that letter Ms. Turnbuckle had given me. After an hour twisting and turning unable to get asleep, I began reading that stupid *Nightmares for Nincompoops* book again.

"I dreamt that letter was a confirmation congratulating me. It read, 'Luigi Fettuccine, it has been confirmed that you have all the matching numbers. In the enclosed envelope, find the following: A round-trip ticket on Qantas including a two-week stay at the Islander Hotel in Sydney, Australia. You'll be the guest of Paul Grogan for three days at his estate, located in the outback. From there, you will hunt wild boar with Paul and several aborigines. Finally, your trip will culminate in a real down-under barbeque. Please call for further instructions.'

"Next thing I knew, I was on board a plane headed for Australia. After landing, I was met by a representative from 'Pushy Steering House.' A limo waited to transport me to the hotel. After check-in, the gentleman escorted me to all the hot spots in Sydney. We went to a park where we watched boxing kangaroos beat the living hell out of some poor guy. I'll give him this though: bloody and bruised, he wouldn't quit. He refused to say *uncle*.

"We visited numerous tourist attractions. Finally, I was taken to the outback to visit with Paul Grogan. The hunting trip into the bush was exciting. The sunsets were breathtaking.

"On my final night, Paul prepared a sumptuous Aussie barbeque. He fired up the barbie, while I relaxed sipping Australian beer. I guess I had one too many. As he prepared the large prawns, I downed another brew. By now, the beer was getting to me as my head began spinning.

"Paul turned to place the shrimp on the barbie, when suddenly, right before my eyes, he transformed into a humongous shrimp. Not believing what I saw, I blinked rapidly several times."

"Please continue, Uncle Louie. You've whet my appetite for more," said Sonny.

"I closed my eyes tightly, hoping it was just a figment of my imagination. Soon I learned it was not. That's when the giant shrimp grabbed hold of me and began peeling off my outerwear, as we so often do to them. Next he swished me around in a pool of ice water. Shivering, my skin became reddish in color. Then he patted me dry with eucalyptus leaves.

"Then I was floated in a giant clamshell containing the most *vile-smelling marinade* imaginable. Trying to keep warm, I curled up directly behind a female shrimp, in a *prawn-ographic* position. After about 30 minutes had passed, the giant shrimp picked me up. Shaking off the excess marinade, he placed me onto a large dish-shaped rock. Lying naked, I began shaking uncontrollably. Then to my disbelief, he picked up a bamboo pole, which had a pointed end. Realizing I was about to be skewered up the wazoo, I began screaming at the top of my lungs.

"Suddenly I heard a calming voice calling, 'Mr. Fettuccine wake up. You're having another nightmare. Don't be frightened. It's only a bad dream.'

"Opening my eyes, I saw an aide standing next to me. The stench that engulfed my room was overpowering. I asked the aide, 'Miss, what is that awful odor?'

"Lifting the covers slightly while peering beneath, she said, 'Mr. Fettuccine, you've messed the bed.' Upset at being accused of such a thing, I shouted, 'I did not. You're probably smelling that stinking *marinade!*'"

"Holy cow, Uncle Louie," said Sonny, "that's the best one yet. I think I know the answer to your problem. It's quite obvious you must stop reading that novel. *Nightmares for Nincompoops* is not for you."

"If I do as you say, Sonny, how the dickens am I going to fall asleep?"

"May I make a suggestion?"

"Sure."

"First, let's get rid of the book. If you still need help falling asleep, why don't you ask H.G. for help? After all, he did say if you need him just call his name, right?"

"Yes," said Louie, "I'll start tonight. Thanks, Sonny, that's a great tip."

Leaving the room, Sonny headed for Ms. Turnbuckle's office. He knocked and entered.

"Hi, Sonny," she said. "How did you make out?"

"I don't think you'll be hearing from my uncle anymore. I'm dropping the book he's been reading off at the library. These stories frightened the heck out of him. Everything should be okay now. If anyone else shows up, they won't stand a ghost of a chance, at least as long as H.G. has anything to say about it…"

"Thank you, Sonny," Ms. Turnbuckle said. As they shook hands, she said, "By the way, who's H.G.?"

"H.G.? Oh, he's just an old crony of my Uncle Louie's. Bye, Ms. Turnbuckle!" Sonny replied as he walked out the door.

Chapter 9
Showtime at Dumpsters

"Sonny, come quick!" screamed Jo.

Imagining the worse, he hurried in the direction of her voice. "Here I come," said Sonny, "are you all right?" Entering the room, still in stocking feet, he stepped in a puddle of water. "What happened?" he asked.

"I don't know," said Jo. "I began filling the hot tub, when I noticed water pouring from beneath."

Removing the door to check, Sonny found the filter hadn't been replaced during the last cleaning, because of his carelessness. Quite upset, Sonny rushed to replace the filter, thus stemming the flow. When done, he began mopping up.

"Leave everything," said Jo, "you can straighten up later. If we don't hurry, we'll be late. It's almost 2:00 p.m."

They were invited to see a show at Dumpsters. Once each month, local talents donated their time to entertain residents at the home. It's a wonderful thing they did for the elderly. Rushing to beat all hell, they barely arrived on time, only to discover the comedian was caught up in the usual Route 80 traffic jam. Twenty minutes had passed, when suddenly sounds of whispering echoed throughout the room, as word spread announcing the comic's arrival. House lights flickered then dimmed, as the pianist played the comic's signature song, "Smile, Darn You, Smile." The curtain opened and out strolled the smiling entertainer. Greeting the audience, he apologized for the delay, assuring the residents that the jokes are done in good taste. After his introduction, the comic began his humorous patter.

"Those of you connected to cath-bags," he said, "smile, for today is your lucky day. As for the rest of you, by the time I'm through, you'll wish you were."

Once the audience got the gist of his remarks, fluid levels began to rise.

"Before continuing, allow me to make a disclosure. My name is Jorge Washington Rabinowitz. I suffer from a terminal illness. My jokes are killing me; don't worry, it's not contagious. I was born in a trunk. At least that's what my father said. He described it in this manner. 'According to

Webster, the trunk is part of the human torso. Although in your mother's case, it was more like a packing crate. After depositing my belongings, she stored them for nine months, 'til time came for your coming out party.'" When the laughter subsided, he continued.

"Remember the old days of Burlesque? They were vaudeville shows that entertained the audience with comedy routines, exotic dancing, and partial nudity." Rabinowitz asked, "How many guys only went to hear the jokes? Raise your hands." Not a single hand went up.

"That's odd," he said, "it's hard to believe not one of you can get it up anymore." That remark got a rise from the men in the audience.

"Do you remember theater security walking up and down the aisle carrying a nightstick, looking for stiffs in the crowd? My horny buddy Sheldon got whacked every time we went.

"It was the job of the baggy-pants comics to tell corny jokes. How can we ever forget those slapstick spoofs? Basically, they followed the same format. They were brief, humorous, satirical skits, involving the *top banana*, a straight man, and a scantily-clad vivacious female. Always a favorite of the mostly male audience was the doctor, nurse, and patient take-off. My all time favorite comic was Cheese-an-Crackers Hagen." That struck a familiar chord with the men.

"Now folks," said Jorge, "listen closely. Do you hear the beat of the bass drum coming from the orchestra pit? Listen!" Mouthing the staccato drumbeat, "*Boom ba da boom, ba da boom, ba da boom.* That my friends, was the cue for the stripper to come out and strut her stuff. First was the third ranking performer, followed by the second. Finally, the one all the guys waited for made her appearance, *the main attraction.* Each stripper had her own synchronized routine. Some worked fast, others slow. The red velvet curtain was a familiar prop. Strippers had signature routines when working the crowd. The mostly male audience began chanting, 'Take it off, take it all off.' That of course was wishful thinking, on their part.

"As I mentioned before, some worked the curtains while others shimmied and shaked their buns faster then a plate of Jello before it gels. On the other hand, headliners had their own styles. My favorite was the captivating enchantress, *Gypsy Rose Lee.* I especially enjoyed when she was grinding and gyrating her voluptuous torso. The men put their hands together in approval. The one thing I was unable to figure out was the *twirling dervish routine.* It made a mockery of the laws of gravity. The stripper covered the nipples of her well-endowed boobs with pasties. Hanging from the pasties were colored tassels. What was truly amazing, was the proficient manner with which she was able to rotate each *knocker* simultaneously in opposite directions. It's what one might refer to as *tit-for-tit.*" With that, the house lit up with laughter. "The Jewish princess I'm married to once took a shot at it, the only problem was she never got past her *schnozz,*" said Jorge. "While on the subject, my wife Goldie had so many face lifts, when she meets her maker, even he won't recognize her.

"Being raised in Essex County New Jersey, the guys I hung with frequented the burlesque houses in Newark. The most famous were the Empire and Minskys. During intermission, the barker stood in front of the main curtain and gave his spiel. Decked in black trousers, a hat, and white shirt with a garter around his sleeve, his job was to make a sales pitch. He usually spoke with a gravelly voice. His pitch went something like this, 'Now listen up gents, for the mere price of fifty cents, one half of one dollar, you can be the lucky recipient of a truly wondrous gift. Folks, the contents to be found within each and every package are guaranteed to amuse and titillate each and every one of you. If not completely satisfied, your money will be refunded. As the beautiful young ladies pass among you, dig deep into your pockets. Take advantage of this once in a lifetime offer. Don't be satisfied with one; get two, three, or more. You won't be sorry! Each bag contains a different prize. I repeat, no two gifts are the same; you will be rewarded with many hours of pleasure.'

"As the scantily-clad strippers walked up and down the aisles, they were accompanied by security. The men holding greenbacks were rewarded with a bag usually containing a small paperback book. Remember guys; we referred to them as dirty books? On each page could be found cartoon characters in the saddle, such as Jigs and Maggie, and Moon Mullins. The faster we flipped the pages, the faster they rode. On occasion, security had to escort a long-handed client from the theater. Their crime was one of trying to cop a cheap feel. As I look over the house, I notice a few of those guys in the audience, so be careful ladies." With that remark, the crowd began laughing. Waiting for the laughter to subside, he continued.

"The other day I paid a visit to the gastroenterologist, complaining of gas. 'Which end?' asked the doctor. 'Both!' I said. 'Seems like you're a candidate for a double ender,' said the doctor. I asked, 'What the hell is a double ender?' The doc said, 'You need both a colonoscopy and endoscopy.'

I said, 'If you plan on doing both at the same time, make sure you don't work *ass-backwards!*'" Again they laughed.

"My urologist handed me a prescription for Viagra, saying I was impotent. Waiting for it to be filled, I walked through the store. High on a shelf, I pulled down a can marked *Niagara.* Recalling Mom used it to stiffen my father's collars, I began scanning the label, which read 'professional finish, crisp classic look, 100 % guaranteed.' Rotating the can, I further read, 'shake well, contents under pressure. Contains 138 spritzes.' I noted the shelf price was $1.38. Running the figures through my head, that worked out to be a penny apiece. Further realizing at my age, one can should last a lifetime. Comparing prices, I opted for the spray starch, figuring if it made pop's *limp* collar stiff, imagine what it could do for me."

Because the cath-bags were cresting, they decided to take an intermission. Returning from the restroom, Louie said, "This old geezer's a riot, he's the best one yet."

"I agree," said Sonny, "he's excellent."

When everyone's tank was on empty, they returned for refills. Once seated, Rabinowitz began where he left off.

"Last evening, I cheated on my former wife. I took my new bride to dinner. The restaurateur stopped at our table inquiring if everything was satisfactory. I said, 'Your house wine is superb, how are sales going?' 'Phenomenal!' He answered. 'We pour 300 glasses a night.' 'That's impressive,' I said. 'How would you like to double your volume?' As his ears perked up, he said, 'Please tell me how.' I said, 'That's easy. *Fill 'em up!'*

"Not a day goes by," said Jorge, "that the news media bombards us with stories of nursing home abuse. My dear mother-in-law was a resident at Lung Island Home for Jews. Abuse there is a daily occurrence. Someone's always getting clobbered. Last week at the behest of the administrator, I was invited to discuss the growing problem. While seated across from his desk he said, 'Things have gotten out of hand.' Sympathizing with his dilemma, I asked, 'Is there anything I could do to help?' Removing his sunglasses, exposing a shiner, he answered, 'Yes, get your mother-in-law the hell out of here, before she kills somebody!'" On that note, Ms. Turnbuckle and Mr. Stuckly, the administrator of Dumpsters burst out laughing, soon joined by the others in attendance. The comedian continued.

"If you like that one, I got plenty more where that came from. Goldie had an uncle Abe who was a resident at a non-sectarian facility. Being somewhat senile, when those of the Catholic persuasion visited the local church, he went along for the ride. Once inside, parishioners stood in line waiting to enter the confessional. Guess what? So did Abe! When his turn drew near, he entered, sat down waiting to do his *duty.* After several minutes passed, a small panel slid open. A voice on the opposite side said 'Yes my son, may I help you?' To wit Abe said, 'Have you got any paper on your side?' Luckily I happened by the church and spotted Abe standing out front looking disoriented. I pulled to the curb, left the car and rushed to his side. Suddenly the church doors opened, as one-by-one parishioners filed out, followed by the priest, who seemed to be gasping for air. Noticing Abe, he walked in our direction stopping to speak with me. He said my uncle shouldn't have gone in the confessional. Apologizing I said, 'I understand completely Father, he's not even Catholic. I hope his going in the confessional didn't cause much of a problem?' The priest, somewhat disturbed, said, 'It would have been better had he gone in the toilet!' Shocked to learn what happened, I asked, 'Father, are you planning to take action?' 'Yes,' he said, 'I'm going to fumigate!' Poor Uncle Abe, since he's become senile he doesn't know *shit from shinola."* The residents roared, as Rabinowitz got ready to fire another salvo.

"There's a good side to everything," said Rabinowitz. "As a direct result of the 1986 Chernobyl nuclear disaster, Ukranian farmers discovered that due to radiation, cucumbers had grown *enormous* in size. In 1999, a former elected official and I received radiation for prostate cancer. Unlike his wife who divorced him, Goldie remains, hoping to see if the *aforementioned benefits* are forthcoming!

"My older brother Sammy's wife, Becky, passed away last year. Ever since, he's been despondent. Both were residents at the same nursing home. One afternoon while sitting in the confines of his room, a new female resident passed his door. Looking in, she noticed him gazing off in space. Wondering why, she knocked on the door and walked in. Approaching the old gent, she said, 'Hello, I'm Sophie. You seem alone, would you like to talk awhile?' Noticing her to be 20 years his junior, he invited her to sit beside him. While doing so, she noticed his zipper was open and the *little guy* was peeping out. As Sammy glanced off in a daze, Sophie attempted to return *it* to its resting place. Upon doing so, he quickly moved, locking her hand in place. Smiling he said, 'Becky my love, you've returned.' Realizing he was hallucinating, she remained still." As the audience sat on the edge of their seats, Jorge continued. "Disregarding her original intent, with her hand fixed, the two struck up a conversation. Thinking he was coming out of his shell, she continued this daily ritual.

"One day she noticed another woman had taken her place. Sophie was beside herself. Crying uncontrollably, she confronted Sammy and asked, 'What does she have that I don't?' Looking off in space, Sammy blurted out, 'Parkinson's.'" Once the laughter subsided, Rabinowitz said, "You've been a wonderful audience. Keep your positive attitude. So what if you forget once in a while. It's no big deal, we all do. Take time to laugh. After I shower, I look in the mirror, and laugh like hell. Above all, *never say uncle.*" He blew a kiss, turned, and walked off.

The thunderous applause was ear shattering. Standing, Louie turned to the gang and said, "This guy's terrific." Everyone agreed. As they left the recreation room, Louie reminded Herman of the meeting pertaining to the fundraiser in the a.m. Jo and Sonny said good-bye, then left the building for their journey home, ready to face the mess they left earlier.

The following morning, Louie called a meeting of the committee. The discussion centered on the subject of the upcoming fundraiser. The roll call included Louie, Herman, the three Pet boys (Max, Moe, and Morris), Dick Furst, Napoleon Jones, Whitey Tubs, Robinson Hood, Pasquale Bone-a-part, Freddie Fish, and Walter Birdbath. America's oldest and brightest decided to have a car wash for their fundraiser. The unique idea was the brainchild of Herman Short. By an eleven to one vote, Louie Fettuccine was nominated chairman. The next closest was Herman Short, who garnered one vote—his own!

After a physical checkup by Dr. Feelfine, Dick Furst, who recently had a change of life circumcision, was listed as questionable. It was a touchy situation but Dr. Feelfine felt, by Saturday, Dick could hold his own.

Under doctor's advisement, the men were asked to refrain from vigorous activities, namely, checkers and crossword puzzles. Pocket pool was permissible.

On Wednesday, Sonny arrived to visit his uncle. The minute he walked in, Louie related the good news. Excitedly he said, "Sonny, guess what! Our troop voted to have a *fun* raiser."

"Excuse me, Uncle Louie, I think you mean a fundraiser," said Sonny.

"Whatever," said Louie. "The event will be a car wash."

"That's original," said Sonny. "If I can be of any help, just name it."

"Thanks Sonny, but this is something we must do ourselves," said Louie. "It will be good for us to earn a buck. You never know when the checks from Social Security might dry up. In any event, we can list the car wash as recent work experience."

"I can see you guys are a determined bunch," said Sonny.

"You betcha," said Louie.

"Would you mind if I dropped by Friday afternoon to see how you're progressing?" asked Sonny.

"Not at all," said Louie, "do that."

"OK, see you then."

When Friday rolled around, Sonny showed up as promised.

"Hi, Uncle Louie! Hi, Herman! How are you guys doing?" asked Sonny.

"Great," said Herman. "Your uncle and I are making last-minute preparations."

"As I drove up, I noticed all the signs had been posted," Sonny said.

"Yes," said Louie, "they were hand-painted by one of the ladies. I think the menu of services she selected has a great deal of imagination," he said. "Don't you?"

Menu

99 cents	Regular Wash
99 cents	Wash and Set
99 cents	Wash and Blow Dry
99 cents	Shampoo Only (Interior)
99 cents	Double Process (Wash and Wax)

10% off Wednesdays-Senior Citizen's Day
Ask about Our <u>Detailing</u>
*Pay first. Out-of-town checks unacceptable!
$20 charge for bounced checks
Manager – Luigi Fettuccine

"Yes," said Sonny, "I've never seen a sign quite like it. By the way Uncle Louie, did you explain you were running a car wash?"

"Of course," said Louie. "Why do you ask?"

"Nothing really," said Sonny, "Who's responsible for the menu selections?"

"Bea Styles," said Herman.

"It's the first time she's done anything like this. Mamie said years ago Bea managed a beauty parlor," said Louie.

"Oh, I see," said Sonny, "that explains it."

Sonny noticed the prices were all the same. "Why are you charging the exact same price for everything?" asked Sonny.

"Lois Price was responsible for that brilliant decision. Before retiring, she operated a discount store," said Louie.

"I see!" said Sonny, scratching his head.

"The entire operation was well thought out," said Louie. "Every detail has been scrutinized."

"May I ask," said Sonny, "how do you expect to make money charging low prices?"

"That's easy," said Louie.

"Two new members recently joined our group. They told us, we'd make it doing volume," said Herman.

"If anyone knows, they should!" said Louie. "Before retiring, they owned a supermarket chain."

"OK, well good luck," said Sonny.

"Wait," said Louie, "there's something else. Bone-a-part, our newest member, was a sanitary engineer at a raw sewage disposal plant. He made up the duty roster."

"Take a look," said Louie, as he handed Sonny the chart.

Dirty Dozen

Herman Short	Roofing
Max, Moe, and Morris Pet	Shampooing
Dick Furst and Freddie Fish	Wheels and rims
Walter Birdbath	Sudsing
Robinson Hood	Trunk
Napoleon Jones Passenger	side doors
Pasquale Bone-a-part	Driver side doors
Whitey Tubs	Vacuuming

"Uncle Louie," said Sonny, "I count eleven names. Where's yours? What's your job?"

"Me? I collect the dough. I told them I was a retired loan shark," Louie said smiling.

Early Saturday morning, the bucket brigade marched out armed with hoses, sponges, soap, and towels. The staging area was located at the rear of the building. The first customer was waiting in line. Louie walked over to greet him, asking what he wanted done.

"Hi!" said the overly friendly gentleman as he emerged from his automobile. Extending his hand, he said, "My name is Joe Washburn. I own Wishy Washy Auto Wash."

"Pleased to meet you," said Louie. "I'm the manager. What can I do for you?"

Looking at the menu he said, "I'll have a wash and blow dry."

"That'll be 99 cents," said Louie.

Handing him a dollar, Washburn said, "Keep the change."

"Thanks," said Louie. "Do you mind if I ask a question? How come you brought your car here? I thought you said you own a car wash."

"Oh I do," said Washburn, "I'm scouting around for workers and I thought I'd check you guys out. Do you mind if I watch?" he asked.

"Not at all," said Louie, "go right ahead."

As the Dirty Dozen began washing their first car, the line of potential customers began forming. At first, there looked to be 25 cars in line, and the operation had only begun. It was still early, but the temperature had already reached 80 degrees. Each member was tackling his job. The Pet boys positioned themselves inside the car and began the shampooing process. The remainder of the group started their assignments. Word that the manager from Wishy Washy Auto Wash was watching encouraged the troop to work faster. Nearly two hours later, Washburn's car was finished. He hopped into it and drove away without saying a word. Louie and Herman were unable to understand why.

As the waiting line grew longer, the next vehicle pulled up. It was a conversion van. Unable to reach the roof, Herman ran in to get a ten-foot ladder from Philly. Ascending the ladder, he climbed on the roof. Once on top, he asked Freddie to hand up a bucket, sponges, and two 36-inch pieces of twine. With none immediately available, he hurried to maintenance to pick up the items. After handing them to Herman, the little guy proceeded to tie two large sponges to the bottoms of his bare feet. Dipping each foot into the soapy solution, he began his skating act, reminiscent of his circus days. As Herman skated across the roof, he asked Louie to turn down the sound of hard rock blasting from inside the van.

To Louie's surprise, he was unable to open any of the doors. The Pet boys were locked in. The driver left the keys in the ignition. As the sound grew louder, Louie cupped his hands, trying to look through the steamed windows. Finally he discovered the answer. The intense heat within the car's interior caused the Pet brothers to fall asleep. In doing so, they were providing a free rock concert.

"Quick, somebody call 911," said Louie. "The Pets have passed out. The doors and windows are locked, I'm worried."

As someone ran to make the call, leaning over the edge, Herman slipped and fell into the large galvanized tub filled with soapy water. With Herman almost drowning, the Pets' future uncertain, Louie pinched himself, checking to see if he was having another nightmare.

In the meantime, the long line faded fast. Nearly five and a half hours had passed since the operation began. Several vehicles, including ones owned by Ms. Turnbuckle and Sonny, remained. The locksmith, who had been summoned, arrived in the nick of time to unlock the door. Once the Pets were freed, Herman said, "See Louie, I guess the SPCA is right when they say on hot days never leave *pets* locked in a car." Louie turned, looked at Herman and began laughing. Dr. Feelfine came running to examine the Pets. Still dripping, Herman said to Louie, "Maybe we should have called a vet instead."

Still laughing, Louie said, "If you think that's funny, you should see the bill the locksmith just handed me for $119.00!"

Another hour passed and the van was finally ready. The driver paid his 99 cents and drove off. Seven hours had gone by as the cleaning crew started on Ms. Turnbuckle's car.

Sonny said, "It's getting late. You guys look exhausted. I'll be back tomorrow. By the way, how much money have you taken in so far?"

"Let's see." Doing the addition in his head, Louie said, "If we add the $1 including tip we made on Mr. Washburn's car and the 99 cents for the van, we took in $1.99. If I were to subtract the $1.99 from the locksmith's bill of $119, we're in a hole for $117.01. There is a bright side, Sonny. A potential customer asked how long it would take to detail his car."

"What did you tell him?" asked Sonny.

"Oh," said Louie, "I asked if he could give us at least six months; we're very fussy!"

"From what I can see," said Sonny, "business is extremely slow, wouldn't you say?"

"No," said Louie, "we are!"

"What do you plan on doing?" asked Sonny.

"Mamie told me one of the girls formerly worked for a professional fundraising company. She strongly advised us to consider some other venture to raise money. I see Mamie walking in our direction carrying the new sign," said Louie. "Wait until you see what it says."

Mamie showed Sonny the sign. It read,

Senior Marathon Dance Contest.

Dance Till You Drop.

Entry fee of $2.

"My friend, Braciole, is judging the event," Louie said.

"You mean the former undertaker?" asked Sonny.

"Yes," said Louie, "don't you think it's fitting he do it?"

As Louie and Sonny ended their conversation, the men entered the building.

"Look who's heading our way," said Louie. "It's Olivia. It's too bad; since she developed Alzheimer's, she's become a wheelchair user. Look how she's able to propel herself using only her feet."

"I'll say," Sonny said, "she can really move along."

"I'm not the least bit surprised," said Louie. "Olivia has the heart of a lion. She'll never say uncle. No doubt, each day things get a little tougher, but she keeps plugging along. Herman told me, last week while standing outside Ms. Turnbuckle's office, Olivia came by. She brushed against his leg with her wheelchair. Ms. Turnbuckle bent over and said, 'Hello Olivia. Do you know who I am?' Olivia looked at her dumbfounded, hesitated a moment, then said, 'No, but if you go into the nurse's office, Ms. Turnbuckle will tell you!'" Herman soon joined the two men.

"Herman," said Louie, "would you mind if I ask a personal question?"

"Not at all, Louie. Shoot," said Herman.

"What were you and Sally arguing about?" Louie asked.

"At times, Sally has a tendency to get a little bitchy," said Herman. "She was squawking that during lovemaking, I scratched her with my long toenails. She told me I'd better cut them. Yesterday the van drove the women to the mall."

"Yes, I know," said Louie. "What's that got to do with your long toenails?"

"Well, you see, I went for a walk. Do you know where the mobile home park is down the street?

"Yes," said Louie.

"As I passed, I saw a sign posted on one of the trailers. It read 'Nails Clipped.' I stopped to talk to the young woman. She told me she's had lots of experience and her prices were reasonable. 'Come in I'll prove it to you,' she said, 'I'll show you how good I am. If you're not completely satisfied, I won't charge you.' After agreeing, I went in. Wouldn't you know, just as I did, the van passed and Sally spotted me. By the way Louie, if you ever need your toenails cut, don't go there."

"Why? Wasn't she any good?" asked Louie.

"That's not it," said Herman, "she's a pro. It's not worth the trouble."

"What happened?" asked Sonny.

"For starters, as soon as I got back, Sally asked, 'What were you doing with that young hussy in the short-shorts?' I said, 'Sally, my sweet, I planned on surprising you.' 'You certainly did, that's for sure!' She cried out, 'All these years, I thought I was the only woman in your life.' Sighing, she further said, 'How could you, you cad! You're nothing but a little cheat.' 'True I'm little, but a cheat, I'm not,' I said. 'I went in to have my toenails clipped. I wanted to surprise you. I didn't want to keep scratching your back during sex.'"

"How did Sally handle that line?" asked Louie.

"I wasn't handing her a line; it was the truth!" said Herman. "Sally said, 'In the first place, if you wanted your nails trimmed, why didn't you ask me?' 'What's the second place?' I asked. 'When that hussy finished clipping your nails, did you try them out on her back?'"

Turning to Louie for some wisecrack response, Herman looked directly at him and said, "Well?"

Pausing a minute, Louie said, "Well, did you?"

With that, the two men smiled, then turned to Sonny and began laughing. Soon they were joined by Sonny, once he realized he was the brunt of still another joke. As Herman ran to meet Sally, Sonny and Louie continued their conversation.

"Uncle Louie," said Sonny, "do you recall telling me, you were once married to the devil's daughter?"

"Of course I do. What makes you ask?" said Louie.

"Oh," said Sonny, "I was wondering, when did you first realize you were?"

"About six weeks into our marriage. Carmela ran down to the supermarket for a quart of milk. Because she was gone so long, returning three hours later, I looked at the milk carton to see if her picture was on it. When I asked what happened, she responded by saying, 'I nearly killed an old lady!' 'With the car?' I asked. 'No, with my bare hands,' she said growling. That was first clue."

"What was the second?" asked Sonny.

Opening the closet door, Louie pulled out an old shoebox, removing a letter. Opening the envelope, he said, "Carmela asked me to mail it, but I forgot. Last night I found and opened it. Would you care to hear what she wrote? Keep in mind this was written almost 58 years ago."

"OK," said Sonny.

"By the way," said Louie, "the letter was being sent to the local newspaper's Letters to the Editor column. I'll read what she wrote:

'Today I came close to killing an old lady. Not with my automobile, but with my bare hands. As every young person knows, rather than go to a supermarket for a quart of milk, it would be quicker to go to a dairy farm and milk a cow.

'The reason I mention this, is milking an old cow at the farm is far easier than trying to get past one in the supermarket. Some old lady stood for hours on end checking every price while blocking the aisle with her shopping cart.

Reminiscent of a cow out to pasture, she stood chewing her cud. By the time I was able to get by her, I was covered with battle scars. If that isn't enough, the old battle-axe didn't even have the decency to apologize. Fear not though, someday I'll see her burn in hell.'"

"Wow!" said Sonny. "I can understand why you feel as you do. I take it that is why you never mailed that horrible letter."

"Yes," said Louie, "that is until now. I added a postscript, which reads: 'P.S. Sir, would you be kind enough to give the devil his due? Please reprint this excerpt.'" Then Louie showed Sonny the postscript which had been signed "Carmela Fettuccine," which was changed by Louie to "Fradiovolo (the devil)."

"There's something else I must tell you," said Louie.

"What's that?" asked Sonny.

"She was fond of deviled crabs, deviled eggs, and devil's food cake," said Louie.

"Now I understand," said Sonny as he glanced at his watch. "It's getting late now, I have to run. I promised I'd take my grandchildren to the movies. See you guys next week."

"Good-bye," said the fellows as Sonny left.

Chapter 10
Revisiting the Good Old Days

Arriving home late Wednesday afternoon, Sonny discovered Jo busy preparing one of his favorite dishes, *pasta fagiolo* (pasta and beans). Using old family recipes and elaborating upon them, she turned out scrumptious, mouth-watering meals. As Sonny entered the kitchen, he walked over to the stove.

"Boy, that sure smells good," he said as he raised the lid and leaned over to take a whiff.

Jo said, "Put back the cover." She scolded him, saying, "Can't you wait 'til it's cooked?"

"Sorry," Sonny said. "It's just that I've worked up an appetite. Uncle Louie and I were having a discussion concerning his mother's cooking."

"Tell me more," said Jo.

"Like you, she never used a cookbook. It was just a pinch of this and a little of that. Her kitchen, located in the rear of their Italian grocery store, was large, but simple, especially by today's standards. There were two stoves: a coal stove for heating and keeping finished dishes warm, and an old-fashioned combination gas stove and oven. The large, porcelain sink had a built-in drain board. In a corner of the kitchen stood a wooden icebox. In the center of the kitchen was a wooden table with carved legs. The table could easily accommodate 25 hungry mouths. The convenient thing about the kitchen being located directly behind the store was that whenever she ran out of any foodstuff, she didn't have far to go. Not only that, the price was right," said Sonny.

"What else did he have to say?" asked Jo.

"He told me back then, Italian families had many things in common. For example, macaroni was the main staple. It was on the menu three times during the week, plus Sunday. Except on Sunday, they fancied it up and called it ravioli or lasagna. *L'insalata*— salad—was always served after the main course, along with the gravy meat. Once the kids grew up, they were surprised to find that homemade Italian cordials and wine could be bought at the local liquor store.

"You know something else he told me Jo, he said, in every room of the house a crucifix hung. Not only that, a figure of a saint stood on guard duty in the front yard. By the age of eight, every kid was taller than their grandmother. Easy to distinguish, she was the one in black, with her hair in a bun, and her stockings rolled down to her ankles. He also told me when he was a kid, everyone in the family understood Italian, even the dog."

"What are you talking about?" asked Jo.

"Well for instance, he said when his father called to their dog. He would say 'Vito, *venire qua,*' (come here). And you know what? Vito ran right over," said Sonny.

Laughing, Jo said, "You know, that's not the first time I've heard that. My grandfather had an Italian bulldog."

"Then he told me about the holidays, which were usually celebrated at his house. On Christmas Eve, his Aunt Elvira and mother cooked the traditional seven fishes. His favorite was *Baccala con patata*—codfish and potatoes—although he loved them all, including the many mouth-watering side dishes. I asked if he ever made *la scarpeta*. 'Are you kidding!' he said, 'wiping your dish clean with a hunk of Italian bread is a must when Italian blood runs through your veins.'

"There was always an abundance of fresh fruits, nuts, especially *castangna* (chestnuts) roasting. He said all the kids loved to break a piece of fennel, using it as a straw to drink down Uncle Salvatore's homemade red wine. The meal usually concluded with freshly brewed *demitasse* (Italian coffee), homemade cordials, and a variety of Aunt Anna Marie's Italian *dolce'* (pastries).

"Once everyone's bellies were filled to capacity, they went off in different directions. While the women cleaned up, men sat around playing *la carta (* cards) and discussing world affairs. The kids were so darn tired, they fell asleep. These preliminaries were in preparation for Midnight Mass. As 11:00 p.m. rolled around, mothers began preparing the kids for the three-block walk to Mt. Carmel, the neighborhood church."

"It was located in Orange, New Jersey, wasn't it?" asked Jo.

Acknowledging her with a nod, Sonny continued. "Uncle Louie said on Christmas Eve, the church was beautifully decorated and brightly lit. Once inside the over-packed building, the heat generated by overstuffed parishioners was overwhelming. Ushers turned on fans, which did nothing more than move stagnant air from one side of the church to the other. He explained one of the Capuchin monks, Father Norbert, was always at the entrance to greet them. To first-time visitors, he was easily distinguishable by his infectious smile slightly hidden beneath an overgrown white beard, which was usually stained."

"What do you mean by stained?" asked Jo.

"He said it was stained with whatever he'd just eaten. He also said when he went into the confessional, at the end, Father would say, 'Now be a good-a boy and say ten-a Hail-a Marys.'"

"Uncle Louie said years ago the church became so packed, they had to put bridge chairs in the aisles. Even with that, latecomers stood on the steps outside, listening to the sermon on loudspeakers. Inside the church, the combination of heat, the smell of fried fish on parishioners' clothing, combined with the odor of silent messengers was nauseating."

"What did he mean by silent messengers?" asked Jo.

"Farts!" said Sonny "There were many varieties. He said each had its own personality. Uncle Louie said the kids assigned different names to them. For example, there was the *sneaker.* It was noiseless, stunk like hell, and hung around a long time. The most significant thing about it was that individuals within range didn't dare look around. That was a sure admission of guilt. Next were the *squealers*. They gave off a loud, shrill sound, which at times were endless. Soldiers referred to them as the 'screaming meemies.' A very unpopular fart was the *wetback*, because it forced the culprits to leave their seats and make a beeline for the john. Embarrassed to no end, they seldom returned. Last, but certainly not least, was what the kids called the *big bang for a buck*."

Laughing, Jo asked, "What the heck was that?"

"That, Jo, was the *piece de resistance*. Just as an individual stretched to drop a buck into the collection basket they let one ride. Literally caught with their pants down, the poor parishioner's face turned beet red, as even the priest looked to see if the ceiling collapsed.

"Previous to Vatican II, Mass was celebrated in Latin. The server usually sang. It was called *le messa cantare,* a singing mass. Long before the 2-1/2 hour celebration was over, the singing lulled the kids to sleep. At the conclusion of Mass, fathers picked up their sleeping charges, carrying one under each arm, and trudged through the snow to return home. Wouldn't you know, the minute they entered the house, the kids begged to stay up so as to welcome old St. Nick. Told he wouldn't come 'til they were fast asleep, they conceded and their mothers put them to bed.

"New Year's Eve was another fun holiday when families joined together partaking of traditional goodies. Once again kids struggled to keep awake 'til the stroke of midnight. With no TV, they played the radio. When midnight arrived, everyone listened to Guy Lombardo and his Royal Canadians play "Auld Lang Syne." Jo have you any idea what it means?" asked Sonny.

"Not really," said Jo.

"Herman told Uncle Louie it's a Scottish lyric which means 'the good old days long past.'

"Uncle Louie said, five minutes before midnight, his father went out in their backyard, loaded his shotgun and at exactly the hour of twelve, fired off two shots. It was a carryover many immigrants traditionally did in the old country. Except his papa did it with flair. He always managed to blast holes in his wife's freshly-washed bloomers, hanging on the outdoor clothesline. When his mother complained, his father would say, 'Why complain, you're the only one in the neighborhood who has air-conditioned bloomers.'

"As soon as things calmed down, they began the big parade. Their makeshift band was outfitted with pots, pans, lids, and spoons. Kids and adults alike marched throughout the house, store, and around the backyard. They sang, laughed, and had one hell of a good time. Looking back, he said, 'It now seems quite silly, but at the time it was wonderful.' I noticed his eyes filled with tears as he said, 'Sonny, we had so much fun.'

"At the conclusion of the night's festivities, they hugged and kissed. Most of all, they gave thanks to the good Lord. Now that he's older, he realizes those were the best times of his life. I said, 'Uncle Louie, what fond memories you have. That's something no one can ever take away.'"

"How true," said Jo, "childhood memories remain forever."

"Sure do," said Sonny.

"Then we took a walk to the cafeteria to get a cup of coffee. There he explained what an old-fashioned wake was like. Before he did, I interrupted to tell him about the wake I went to last Thursday. I told him about Nick's passing and how surprised I was to find that other than his wife, no one else was at the funeral home. I told him the only thing present, other than Nick's wife, was the casket and a small floral piece. I said, 'You know, Uncle Louie, that really bothered me to think none of his family or friends came to pay their respects.' As I excused myself for interrupting, Uncle Louie said, 'Times have changed since he was a youngster.'

"In the old days, the body was laid out in the person's home. Uncle Louie said his mother's friend's wake was held in their home. It reminded him of a motion picture epic. Her body was hardly cold when the door opened and in walked the director. He worked out of his studio, arriving on the set; he carefully read the script to family members before he summoned the prop men. Upon arrival, they began preparing the stage.

"Agreeing the parlor would be used as the staging area, the crew did a complete makeover of the room. Mrs. Scorcha's plastic-covered overstuffed couch, matching fan-back chairs, hammered leather-top cherry mahogany tables and *cappa il monde* lamps were squeezed into an offstage room. The maroon throw rug, bordered with gold fringe tassels, was rolled up and tied with a piece of old clothesline. It was carried to the back hall and thrown down the stairs. Most likely, that's where the name 'throw rug' came from. Once the set had been cleared, beautiful hardwood floors were exposed to complement the hammered tin ceiling.

"The prop men brought in the director's chairs, with his name clearly etched in the wood. They were placed around the perimeter of the theater. Box seats, located immediately adjacent to the star, were reserved for family members. Front row center was set aside for close relatives. Immediately behind were chairs for the potential sidewinders."

"Hold on, Sonny. What's a sidewinder?" asked Jo.

"They were wanna-be fans who attend anyone's wake just to be seen. At the opportune time, the sidewinders would make their move. As a family member left to visit the restroom, the sidewinder rushed to that empty seat. They'd sit sideways, prepared to get up as soon as the previous occupant returned. Sitting that way made it easier to do so.

"With the arrival of opening night, the makeup artist and costumers prepared the star. When finished, she was placed center stage. Included in the casket was a collection of her memoirs. In the kitchen-commissary, family members prepared a light repast of *antipasto* and *lasagna*. Homemade wine was served to toast the star. Her attire was black on black. Family members also wore black, doing so for as long as a year after the star's retirement.

"As show time approached, the lighting crew brought down the house lights. Once the doorman opened the front door, fans rushed in. They also wore black, in respect to the star. When inside they approached her, offering words of adulation, while at the same time, checking to see if their floral pieces arrived. If unable to find them, they would shout across the room to one another, 'Have you seen my flowers?' In response, someone would answer, 'No, I don't see yours, do you see mine?' After that problem was resolved, they sat in their assigned seats. Once the cast was in place, the silence was broken. The sound effects turned up as stand-ins, hired to act out the crying scenario, arrived on the scene. They abruptly left after the director informed them they were on the wrong set. Shortly thereafter, they were heard performing on the back lot.

"After three days of nonstop performances, the producer decided it was time to take the show on the road. Family and fans left the facility and entered their vehicles. The star was carried out by extras and placed into the hearse. The entire party followed suit, entering limos. The entourage was whisked away to the Hollywood Memorial for the final curtain.

"At the conclusion, as the star was laid to rest, without warning, her sister, she had not seen for 40 years, attempted to steal the limelight. By now, the star was in over her head. Looking to upstage her, the sister began screaming, 'I love you. Why did you die?' She flung her body across the casket as it was being lowered. Family and friends were horrified, with the exception of the star's husband. As the casket hit bottom, he pleaded with the ground crew to shovel on the dirt.

"The sister was nominated for female actress in a leading role. She was sure to win the Oscar. The husband was up for male star in a supporting role."

"Was her sister able to climb out at the closing?" asked Jo.

"Yes, but not for long, she went back for a return engagement."

"You mean she died," said Jo.

"Yes," said Sonny. "Her contract had a non-escape clause with a different plot."

"Today, that's known as a sequel," said Jo.

"Whatever," said Sonny.

"Then Uncle Louie asked how I was able to find out where he was living. I told him it was sheer luck. I explained to him, my good buddy, Carmen, through his wife, found out he was a resident at Dumpsters. I told him there was a time I almost thought of quitting, but something inside drove me on to *never say uncle*. It was that strong determination that led me to Dumpsters and him. Uncle Louie told me a related story regarding his grandfather. He said whenever he faces adversity, he remembers it."

"Would you tell me the story? I'd be interested in hearing," said Jo.

"Why not?" asked Sonny. "He said when his grandfather was first married, they lived in the little town of Monte Virgine, high in the Italian Alps. It was there his grandparents raised their family. Many of their neighbors were resentful of his success. No matter what his grandfather did, they were envious. He told me he nearly threw in the towel and left. Instead he refused to quit, or say uncle."

"People are funny that way," said Jo.

"One day, Uncle Louie said, my grandfather told his oldest son, '*Figlio mio* (my son), fetch *l'asino* (the jackass). We must travel to the next town; my dear brother is dying. We must pay our respects.' As his son brought out the beast, my grandfather mounted it. His son preferred to walk in front holding the reins.

"As they passed their neighbor's property, they overheard him say to his wife, 'Look at Fettuccine. He sits on his ass while the poor little boy pulls the beast.' As the day grew warmer, they decided to switch positions.

"A little further down the road, they heard two men talking. One said, 'That poor ailing old man. He walks in the hot sun, while his strong young son just sits on his ass.'

"Hearing that, they both climbed on the animal. Passing a blacksmith's shop, the smithy yelled out, 'How could you be so cruel on such an arid day? While you two sit on your ass, the poor beast is foaming at the mouth!'

"Heeding his remarks, they got off their ass, took the reins and walked in front. His son cut out ear holes and placed his hat over the head of his ass.

"Uncle Louie said his grandfather told him the moral of the story is, *don't make an ass of yourself in order to please others. The envious will never change, once an ass, always an ass.*"

"You know Sonny, your uncle Louie's grandfather was a smart cookie for telling his son that story," said Jo.

Chapter 11
It's Only Business

"Hi, Uncle Louie, this is Sonny. I'm calling to see if you'd like to take a ride, I'm bringing my car in for an oil change."

"Sure," said Louie, "I have nothing special to do today. What time will you be over?"

"Could you be ready in an hour? While there, I want to look at the new models."

"Sounds good to me. I'll let Ms. Turnbuckle know you're picking me up. I'll be waiting out front. See you in a little while, Sonny. Bye."

"Bye, Uncle Louie," Sonny said.

After breakfast, Louie went to tell Ms. Turnbuckle his nephew was picking him up. It looked to be a bit windy, so he decided to go to his room to pick up a jacket. Then he waited at the front door for Sonny to arrive. He came on time.

As they drove away, Louie asked Sonny, "Isn't this a new Caddy?"

"It's two years old. I'm giving it to Jo. We definitely need a second vehicle."

"Kids today sure are lucky," said Louie. "It seems like only yesterday when I think back to the day Papa let me drive his produce truck on my first date.

"When I was 19, I couldn't afford the right time, let alone a new car, for that matter, any car. I can still see the look on Carmela's father's face when I pulled in front of his house in West Orange to pick her up. I hopped out of the truck, walked over to say hello, and introduced myself. He was cutting grass at the time. When he noticed me, he stopped the engine to say hello. After shaking hands, he asked where I parked. 'Right there,' I said, pointing to the truck. He looked in disbelief; the thought that someone would pick up his little girl in a produce truck never entered his mind.

"Because it was our first meeting, not wishing to offend my boyish pride, he calmly said, 'Louie, it's Louie, is that right?' 'Yes sir, Mr. D, I said. 'I was wondering, do you have another means of transportation at your disposal?' he asked. 'Yes sir,' I said. 'Now that you mention it, my friend Dario's father is a sanitary engineer.' 'You mean he's a garbage man?' asked

Mr. D. 'That's right,' I said, 'he has a small truck I can borrow. On second thought, that wouldn't be such a good idea. The slogan on the side of the truck says *One Man's Junk Is Another Man's Treasure.'* As Mr. D's face turned beet red, I thought for sure he'd bust a gut. He bent down to pick up his jacket, which had been lying on the stoop. I turned white as a sheet when I saw him reach into his pocket. I thought he was pulling a rod. Under my breath, I began to say a *Hail Mary.* Boy, was I relieved when I saw him pull out a set of car keys. As Carmela came out, he handed them to me and said I could use his car.

"As we started for the vehicle, he said, 'Louie, in the future, if you expect to date my Carmela, beg, borrow, or steal a car.' 'Yes sir, Mr. D, I promise.' I said. Hurriedly, we hopped into his big Packard and drove off.

"After that, I borrowed my older brother Silvio's car. Sometimes I double-dated with my buddy and his girl. Frankie had a 1930 Essex that was a real piece of work. The battery was located under the floorboard. In order to start the engine, I had to crank it about ten times while he pulled the choke. Until it ran smoothly, it would sputter and spit."

"Uncle Louie, you were probably better off with your father's produce truck," said Sonny.

"You said a mouthful. One night as we drove home from a local joint called the Viking located in Clifton, New Jersey, it started to pour. Frankie's Essex had a canvas roof. The edges where the metal joined the canvas had to be tarred once a month. Guess what good old *Cheech* forgot to do? Because of that, when the fury of the wind picked up the canvas ripped away from the metal, leaving the four of us completely exposed to a torrential downpour. Unable to see because of the heavy rain, Frankie pulled over to the roadside. Carmela and Philomenia began to panic, crying uncontrollably, adding to our dilemma.

"'Quick,' I said. 'Get out of the car. About half a mile back I thought I saw an old farmhouse. Come on; let's make a run for it. It's our only chance.' Frankie said, 'What about my car?' 'With some luck,' I said, 'maybe the river will overflow and wash it away. Let's go! We're wasting time.' Taking hold of the girls' hands, we made a mad dash for the farmhouse.

"Halfway there, an old farmer passing in a truck saw us and pulled over. He rolled down the window and asked where we were headed. After we told him our destination, the old farmhouse ahead, the farmer said, 'Don't bother; it's floating down the river.' 'What are we supposed to do now?

Frankie's car will probably meet the same fate.' I said. 'Quick,' the farmer said. 'We haven't much time. Get into the truck.'

"We helped the two girls into the front seat next to the farmer. Then he advised us to hop in the back and hide under the tarp. With no other choice, we did as he said. As we pulled the tarp over us, hiding from the rain, the farmer's pigs greeted us. The smell was stifling."

"Gee," said Sonny, "that must have been awful, but at least you were safe."

"Sonny, have you ever smelled pigs after they've farted? The stench is overpowering, to say the least. Relying on Carmela to direct the farmer to her home, we arrived just as the rain subsided. As the farmer's truck pulled in front of her residence, Mr. D came running out to meet us. Frankie and I crawled out from under the tarp, covered in pig shit, smelling like a septic tank that backed up.

"Mr. D opened the truck door, helping the girls out. We walked over to the driver's side to thank the farmer. 'That's quite all right,' he said. 'Glad to help; you kids were right in the thick of it.' I thought, 'No truer words have ever been spoken.' 'Good-bye sir, we owe you our lives!' the girls yelled as the farmer pulled away.

"'Hurry, get into the house before you catch your death,' said Mr. D. As the four of us started into the house he yelled, 'Not you guys; you smell like a sewer. Wait for me in the garage.'

"As Carmela's mother attended the girls, Mr. D came into the garage to check us out. Fearful of upsetting him, I began apologizing. 'No need to apologize,' he said. 'No one but God has control of the elements. I will say this, Louie. I think you really outdid yourself this time.' 'What do you mean?' I asked. 'A pig truck! You dated my Carmela in a pig truck!' Unable to keep a serious face, he began laughing. Frankie and I looked at each other in amazement and joined in. 'Here,' he said, while he continued chuckling, 'put on this dry clothing. When you're ready, I'll drive you home.'

"From that day forward, Mr. D's attitude toward me changed, for the better."

"Uncle Louie, when you were first married, did Carmela work?"

"Yes she did. Things were tough back then, so she had to help out. She hopped from job to job, always with an eye to the future. Each new venture ended in disappointment! It wasn't till later in our marriage she found her niche."

"What happened?"

"It was a stroke of genius; Carmela came up with a great concept. As far as we knew, there was no other business quite like it."

"What was the premise behind it?"

"Quite simple indeed," said Louie. "First, let me ask you a question. Other than a physical problem, what do you think is the leading killer of individuals?"

"Stress!" replied Sonny.

"That's right. Now tell me, what is the main reason for stress?"

"Oh, I don't know. Hmm, let me see. Wait! I'd say it has to be worry."

"You're exactly right! That was the basis of her new venture. Everybody worries. If not about health, it's their jobs, money, children, parents, taxes, and so on. People worry about everything. Worry gets in the way of everyday living."

"You know, Uncle Louie, you certainly are right. I never gave it much thought till now. Did Carmela have a name for her business?"

"Yes, she did! It was quite unique: *Worry Warts, Inc.* This was her idea. She'd contact everyday folks by mail, explaining that if they dialed 'LET-MEL-HELP' or 538-635-4357, they wouldn't have to worry anymore. She'd worry for them. In that way, they'd be able to carry on a normal life without a worry in the world."

"How did it work?" asked Sonny.

"Simple. The customer would dial the Worry Warts number, which in turn activated an answering device. I still recall the message. It went like this, said Louie.

'Hello, Worry Warts, thanks for calling. If you're calling because you're worried, relax. Listen to the following prompts. Our menu has been changed to offer the following options. Don't worry. Just listen after the pause. Press "1" if you're worried about everyone but yourself. Press "2" if you're worried about things that shouldn't concern you. Press "3" if you worry about every little thing. Press "4" if you're worried about everything under the sun. Press "0" if you'd like this menu repeated. If you're worried you might forget, stay on the line to be transferred to the first worry-free operator. Above all, don't worry; your call will be answered in three minutes.'"

"Wow," said Sonny, "that was really unique. How did you feel about the new business?"

"At first I was worried she might worry herself to death. After I thought it over, I said to myself, 'What am I worried about?'"

"Did she have trouble finding clients?"

"You've got to be kidding. In no time at all, the phone was ringing off the hook. Business was booming. Carmela was forced to hire more operators. She had new phone lines installed to handle all the calls. She instructed new employees to take a subtle approach, while at the same time putting the clients' minds at ease.

"When the operators answered the phone, they'd say, 'What the hell are you worried about?'"

"Didn't that upset the customers?" Sonny asked.

"Not at all. The answer shocked them into submission, in turn relaxing them. Through aggressive marketing and a strong ad campaign, people began calling Worry Warts, day and night. Soon our garage became overcrowded. Larger quarters were needed. Carmela had to hire still more operators. Expenses were escalating what with advertising, payroll, and the addition of 800 lines. The whole concept was beginning to backfire on Carmela as she began worrying herself sick."

"That's too bad, Uncle Louie, especially with the lucrative business she had going. She must have made a bundle of money."

"Money? What money? Customers paid only if she found an answer to their problem. For hard as she tried, with the exception of her own dilemma, she couldn't come up with a practical solution for anyone."

"What did she do to end her worries?" asked Sonny.

"Claimed bankruptcy!" said Louie.

Upon reaching the dealership they went in. Sonny checked to see if he could have the oil changed. He was pleasantly surprised to learn there was only a 20-minute wait. To pass the time, they went into the showroom to look at the latest models. They spent a half hour looking at the new cars before heading back to Dumpsters. On the way, their discussion continued.

"From what I can see, Uncle Louie, it seems you had your hands full while married to Carmela," Sonny observed as they left the dealer's lot.

"Nobody knows! Only God. For more years than I care to remember, I tried to convince Carmela to take up golf. Finally, one morning as I came down to breakfast, she said, 'Honey, I'm ready!' Immediately I thought, 'Ready for what?' The last time I remember her saying 'Honey, I'm ready,' was on our wedding night. I thought, 'Uh oh. Can it be the love bug bit her?' So I said, 'Ready for what? What are you ready for, Carmela?' 'Golf,' she replied. 'Golf?' I said. 'Did I hear right? I've been trying to get you to learn for over 30 years. Now out of a clear blue sky you say you want to play golf?' 'Yes, Louie, that's right,' she said, 'all my club girls play, with the exception of me.' 'OK,' I said. 'If you're serious I'll make arrangements with the golf pro to give you a few lessons.'

"Carmela went over to Mountain Manor Golf Club to begin. Of course, as all women know, in order to play golf, they must be in vogue. Keeping up with her club girls, she purchased a new set of clubs, a bag, balls, tees, shoes, an umbrella, a glove, three blouses, three sets of shorts, and a cap. That afternoon when she arrived home, she handed me a bill for $1,000. Once I picked myself off the floor, I said, under my breath of course, 'It's alive! It's alive! I've created a monster!'"

"I guess you learned your lesson, Uncle Louie?" ribbed Sonny.

"Well, not quite! I was a glutton for punishment. I made arrangements with my sister, Gen, and husband Harry to play a round of golf at Mountain Manor. They were coming up Sunday evening. Our tee time was for Monday morning. To our disappointment, they had a change of plans. Because I'd already committed to a 9 a.m. tee time, we had to show up. The day began when Carmela woke me at 5 a.m. I pleaded with her to turn off the light, which fell on deaf ears. 'Have you forgotten?' she said. 'We're playing golf.' Looking at the clock, I said, 'I know, but its only 5 a.m., our tee time is at 9.' Knowing better than to get into an argument, I said, 'O.K., O.K.' as I dragged my ass out of bed and staggered, half-asleep, into the bathroom to get my aching bones ready for the unforeseeable.

"Once our golfing equipment was in the trunk we set out for the links. We arrived two hours before tee time, and decided to have a bite of breakfast in the clubhouse."

"How did Carmela look in her golf outfit?" asked Sonny.

"Well," said Louie, "the only thing missing was the calliope."

"What do you mean?"

"In the circus, when the lead clown shows up dressed in a purple and red polka-dot blouse wearing orange and green shorts, and a bright yellow cap topped with a blue tassel, that's one thing. But when she puts on hot pink socks inside kelly green golf shoes, the only thing missing is a calliope," said Louie. "Her outfit caused every head to turn!

"After tipping the attendant for strapping our bags onto the cart, I got in. But not Carmela; she insisted on re-strapping her bag, claiming when golfing, you should make a concerted effort to follow the rules. She said, 'It says so in the book.' To this day, I still don't know what the hell she was talking about. Like I said, I didn't feel like arguing with her. I got out of the cart to buy a Hershey bar. When I returned, I found her behind the wheel, so I walked around the opposite side. Of course, it meant my clubs were behind her and hers were behind me. Oh, well!

"As we pulled away she turned to wave to a couple of club girls, making sure they took notice. Her head was turned and her foot pressed firmly on the pedal. By the time I had a chance to warn her, she rear-ended the cart in front, which had been waiting to move up to the first tee. In anticipation, I covered my eyes. The gentleman got out and walked over to register his rightful complaint. Uncovering my eyes, as luck would have it, it was our insurance agent. Cringing, my face red as the planet Mars, I exited the cart, offering both my hand and apologies. As we exchanged friendly conversation, I turned to find Carmela going ahead of Mr. Bonner. Now doubly embarrassed, I was at a loss for words."

"My goodness, I could just imagine how you felt," said Sonny.

"Not only that," said Louie, "but to this day, I still believe when our rates jumped on the anniversary of our auto policy, it was due to Carmela's reckless driving."

"What happened after that fiasco?"

"My play became erratic. When my time came to tee off, my ball hit a vehicle."

"You mean a golf cart?" Sonny asked.

"No, I sliced it! The ball collided with a passing bus on the nearby highway. In true tradition of golfers everywhere, looking for any excuse, I laid blame on my partner. Due to the passing of Mulligan, I took a Schwartz. Once again, I teed up another ball. As my back was turned, I failed to notice Carmela had driven the cart ten feet forward of the tee. Just as I swung down violently at the ball, Carmela trying to purposely distract me, said, 'Look, there's a double breasted seersucker, nestled in the tree.' When she did, I shanked the ball. As I did, I heard someone scream. The errant ball struck her right thigh. Once settling down, she called me a few choice words. I offered my profound apology, which fell on deaf ears. Now, as her time approached, Carmela teed her ball. While addressing it, she went through the full gamut of body gyrations, swinging through the ball at least five times as if it were my head. Finally connecting, she lofted the ball some 165 yards down the middle of the fairway. I was astounded as she turned and flipped me the bird."

"I guess the lessons paid off?" said Sonny.

"Wait, I'm not done. Let me tell you about the golf cart we drove in. It had absolutely no cover to protect us from the elements. As we approached the tee, it was encircled by water. Carmela drove, I mean literally drove, into it. I rolled up my slacks, removed my footwear, and than stepped into the muddy water. Just as I positioned myself behind the cart, ready to push, without warning, Carmela gunned it, causing me to fall flat on my face in the mud."

"What a fiasco," said Sonny.

"You ain't heard nothing," said Louie. "When we got to the third tee, Carmela's bag was missing. You know, the one she insisted on re-strapping? As she became anxious, I said, 'The bag most likely came loose and dropped off.'

"Circling the cart without concern for the oncoming foursome, she put the pedal to the metal. We flew down the middle of the fairway, unconcerned for life or limb. Balls were whizzing overhead. Finally we arrived back to find her bag lying on the fairway. I got out. As I secured her bag in place, it began raining. 'Quick,' she blurted, 'Louie, get my new umbrella.' I opened it, got into the cart, and held it over our heads. 'No, no, you idiot! It's not for us. Cover my new clubs!' she yelled. 'What about us?' I said. 'What about us? It's only a little water,' she said. Following her directions, I covered the bag as we drove back to the third tee.

"Once again on our merry way, a draft caught hold of the umbrella, launching it into the crotch of a mighty oak. Several attempts to free her "bumbershoot," using the ball retriever proved futile. As lightning danced around us, I attempted to climb the tree. After reaching my target, I started to descend with the umbrella in hand. Suddenly I heard a ripping sound. 'What could that be?' I wondered. My question was soon answered, as I felt a cool, wet breeze fanning my bare rump. 'Hurry, Louie!' Carmela shouted. 'I want to play out the course.' Biting my lip, I said, 'Yes, my dear, here I come.'

"By now, all other golfers had the good sense to leave; but not us. Carmela would never say uncle. We completed all 18 holes. Making our way back to the clubhouse, we were freezing cold and completely soaked. Darkness had set in over the course. The thought of a hot bowl of soup entered my mind. As we approached the clubhouse, there wasn't a soul in sight. 'Hurry, Louie, go knock on the door,' she said. When I got to the top of the stairs, posted on the door the sign read, 'Open 6 a.m. to 6 p.m.' Looking at my watch, I saw it was 8 p.m. That's when it first struck me."

"What's that?" Sonny asked.

"That day should go down in the *Guinness Book of Records* for having played the longest round of golf ever recorded—11 hours. Once our gear was packed in the trunk, Carmela asked, 'Would you like me to drive, Louie?' 'No,' I said, 'Carmela, I think you drove me quite enough today. You must be exhausted.'

"On our way home, Carmela said, 'Thank you, Louie. Today was so much fun. I can't wait till we play again next week. I'm looking forward to it.' 'Me too,' I said, as I popped a nitro."

"By the way, Uncle Louie, when you were actively playing, what was your handicap?" asked Sonny.

"Carmela!" replied Louie.

"Did you get to play together often?"

"Only on our honeymoon. Just kidding! Thank God! After that episode, she played with her club girls," said Louie. "She became really good, and shot in the 90s."

"How many years has it been since her passing?"

Removing his cap, while holding it over his heart, he said, "Carmela bit the dust 15 years ago today."

As they pulled up outside of Dumpsters, Louie said, "Before I go in, Sonny, I'd like to read you a letter I found in my junk box this morning. I received it shortly after we married. Every once in a while, I like to read it."

"And…weep?" asked Sonny.

"No. Laugh," said Louie.

The Letter

"'My Dearest Carmela,

I would like you to know, ever since I first saw your reflection in the lake at Orange Park; I've remained a distant admirer of yours. Your present husband, Louie, must be a real nut to let you out in public alone. For you are, without a doubt, the most gorgeous vision of female pulchritude my eyes have ever seen. If you were my beloved, I would place you on a pedestal for everyone to behold. Your every wish would be my command. I would lavish you with any reward your intelligent mind could conjure up. Sumptuous meals with exotic wines served at five-star restaurants would be commonplace. Unlimited credit cards issued by every high-priced establishment worldwide would be available to you. A chauffeur-driven Rolls Royce would be at your disposal. Around-the-world trips, lasting three months or more, would be a yearly occurrence. Million-dollar houses in several countries worldwide, built by famous architects, would be accessible. All these and many other pleasures of life would be yours my dearest Carmela, should you tire of your present husband.

Respectfully Yours,

— - - - - - - - - - - - - - - - - - -

"Uncle Louie, were you able to figure out who Aunt Carmela's secret admirer was?"

"As a matter of fact, Sonny, I did. After Carmela passed away, I was gathering her belongings and discovered her secret diary. Tucked inside was a brief note. It read,

'Don't forget to write a letter to Louie so he realizes what a wonderful bargain he got when he married me. I'll have to do it later. I must run. Louie is taking me out to the White Castle for a burger.

C.F.

P.S. Don't forget. Lay it on thick!'"

Chapter 12
I Surrender Dear

"Uncle Louie, Uncle Louie," yelled Sonny, "I'm over here!"

Turning to find where the voice originated from, he spotted Sonny scurrying across the parking lot. He noticed he was holding a package in his hand.

Handing it to Louie, Sonny said, "Jo baked chocolate biscotti with roasted filberts for you."

"My favorite," said Louie. "How did she know?"

"I told Jo Grandma made them for you all the time," said Sonny. "My mother had Grandma's recipe and gave it to me. The other day, I found it in an old shoebox, with other treasured memories. Jo thought you might enjoy them."

"Are you kidding? Boy oh boy, I'm going to eat one right now," said Louie.

Opening the bag, he reached in, pulled out the delicacy, broke off a piece, and popped it into his mouth. As he began munching, the sheer ecstasy on his face combined with the muffled oohs and ahs, signified his delight.

Speaking with his mouth full, Louie said, "Come, let's go inside and talk."

Entering the building, Sonny followed Louie onto the veranda where the two sat down.

"When I got home last Wednesday, I couldn't help thinking about Carmela's letter. She must have been a real buster!"

"You'd better believe it!" said Louie. "Hey don't get me wrong. Every marriage has its share of trials and tribulations. Though, with some degree of effort by both parties, they can be resolved. It takes two to tango." Smiling, he said, "Although in our case, Carmela was usually the antagonist!

"Let's face it, women are beautiful creatures men would find it difficult living without. They were put on the planet for many reasons, but their specialty is breaking balls," said Louie. "It's the same the world over.

"Let me give you a few examples. Carmela would always tell me I never listened when she talked! Oh, oh. I see you're smiling, Sonny.

"Lest we forget, here's another beauty. 'Change that station. I can't take anymore of their blabbering. They talk about the same thing over and over. Now I want to watch my program!' In the first place, I honestly never knew the crap she watched were *her* programs. If we had an appointment, I'd ask, 'What time did you say we had to be there?' 'I only told you five minutes ago,' she'd scream. 'You never pay attention, you're always listening to those blabbermouths.'"

"It's uncanny," said Sonny, "that's exactly what Jo does. I'm in the middle of listening to something that's occupied my attention when she decides to talk to me. Obviously I'm not paying attention if I'm listening to something else."

"I know exactly what you mean," said Louie. "Sonny, I'm going to make you bed-wise."

"You mean street-wise, don't you?" asked Sonny.

"No, no. When you get home tonight, in a nonchalant way, ask Jo if your snoring is keeping her awake."

"To be honest with you, Uncle Louie, now that you mention it, lately she's stopped complaining," said Sonny.

"I thought so. Have you ever wondered why?" he asked.

"Not really," said Sonny.

"Well in that case, now is as good a time as any to make you aware of an extraordinary phenomenon known as *sleep apnea final frontier*.

"Getting back to the reason for her not complaining anymore about your snoring, the answer is obvious. You've been tuned out. The truth of the matter is she has reached a much higher frequency than you.

"There's one way to verify it, hit the sack shortly after she dozes off. Please do not be misled by the sound of silence, it's just the lull before the storm. It's the norm for any approaching tempest.

"This is what you can expect as she passes through each phase. First there will be heavy breathing, then puffing, which eventually starts a fluttering sound as the mouth closes. With nowhere for the trapped air to escape, it creates what I call *flutter puff*. Turning from side to side, she suddenly does the unthinkable and rolls on to her back. Once in this freefall state, all hell breaks loose as the volume escalates due to the addition of woofers and tweeters, creating a mix that mimics the sonic boom of an F-18 crashing the sound barrier, reaching the speed of Mach III."

"Now that you've brought it to my attention, I seem to recall loud outbursts such as you've described, but I was under the assumption they were passing planes in the night. Tonight I'll do as you suggest to see if I can catch her in the act."

"Hold on a minute, my boy," said Louie. "There is one caveat. Once you venture on this witch hunt, you may never get a good night's sleep again; for you will go where no man has gone before. Let me also warn you not to be misled by what I refer to as the silence of the lamb. For three whole minutes, there's not a peep. At first you wonder, my God, is she still alive? Soon your thoughts will change to, 'Peace at last, peace at last. Thank God there's peace at last.' But once the armistice is over, that fragile peace will erupt into World War III, as a constant barrage of heavy artillery breaks out, forcing you to go undercover. Don't be tricked into false security. Evacuate the area even if it means retreating to the guest room. Although I must say if you're a light sleeper, no matter where you run, you'll find no sanctuary 'cause sound, like light, travels. No obstacle placed between you and the source will muffle it.

"Don't make this faux pas the next morning by telling her you were awake all night, 'cause as soon as you do, she'll want to know why, even though she already surmises your answer. If you try to resist, she'll press the issue. If you give in and say it's because she snored so loudly she raised the roof off the house, this will be her answer. 'You're just saying that,' or 'You're crazy.' Then, not wishing to accept the facts, she will go on the offensive. 'How about when you snored?' she'll ask. That in itself will prove my theory. Due to her enthusiastic snoring, she cannot hear you anymore. Remember, from that moment on, you will never get a good night's sleep again unless you sleep outside in the doghouse. Oh yes, before I forget, in her mind she's thinking, 'Baby, it's payback time.'

"Be on the lookout for this one. Carmela had a fetish. It seemed like every time I picked up the newspaper and headed for the bathroom to catch up on some serious reading, she'd begin knocking on the door. 'What are you doing in there? You've been in there 20 minutes. When are you coming out? How can you stay in there so long?' When she's finished, I'd answer, 'I'm here because nature called. Before you disturbed my thought, I was reading an article about the problem the city's having with people *dumping* in the park. Furthermore, I'll be out when I'm good and ready. I don't tell you how long to take; why must you tell me?' Of course the door was bolted. To myself I'd think, 'I can't even take a shit in peace.' 'When I go to the bathroom, I'm in and out. I don't sit there,' she'd answer. I'd think to myself, 'I don't blame you, I wouldn't either!'

"Uncle Louie, I guess all men have the same problems in common," said Sonny.

"Without a doubt. Every time Carmela watched her program, after about 20 minutes, her eyelids would droop and soon she'd be fast asleep. That's when I'd pick up the remote, turn the volume down and switch channels. Ten minutes later, her eyes opened and she'd ask why I changed her program and to put it back on. When I told her she was sleeping, she responded, 'No I'm not. I'm just resting my eyes. I heard everything they were saying.'

"Of course Sonny, men are not without fault. According to us, we're never wrong; we know everything. For that same macho reason, we never put down the toilet seat. On that last point, our wives are right to complain. In the middle of the night, that rim gets pretty cold.

"What about the elusive frog that constantly seems to settle in our throats? When I was in the process of trying to rid myself of that little rascal, Carmela would say 'sounds like feeding time at the zoo.' True we snore a little, and yes we even break wind, but as women get older, they too join the party.

"Sonny, take some advice from an old warrior. If you want to maintain a peaceful co-existence, don't think you're always right. Once in a while, whisper these three little words into her ear; 'I was wrong.' She'll love you for it," said Louie.

"By the way Uncle Louie," said Sonny, "what's with the dreams? Are they a thing of the past since you stopped reading *Nightmares for Nincompoops*?"

"Yes and no," said Louie. "Only last evening, after a long dry spell, I had one. Maybe it's because the Easter holiday is approaching,"

"Tell me about it," said Sonny.

"Let me see. Last night for supper we had cream cheese, lox, and bagels. It didn't sit well with me; I had an upset stomach till around 3:00 a.m.; that's when I must have fallen asleep. Once I went off, it began.

"Somehow or other, I found myself walking through the streets of downtown Jerusalem. I was decked out in a long tattered robe, with sandals on my feet, sporting long black hair, with beard to match. A rope, with a placard attached, hung from my neck. Printed in Hebrew, was 'Number One.' In my hand, I held written instructions, which read as follows:

'Number One, you are to proceed to the corner of Market and Main Streets. There you'll find a tailor shop operated by Moe Swartz. Your appointment, Number One, is for 10:00ish. After entering the shop, if Moe is not present, just call out 'Moe are you in?' Then wait for his response. Please, Number One, do not read further till you're passed this threshold.'

"Following the instructions, I proceeded to my destination. After a ten-minute walk, I arrived at the designated spot. There I saw the sign 'Moe Swartz, Tailor.' After entering the establishment, I closed the door. With no one present, according to instructions, I called out, 'Moe, are you in?'

"A voice from the back room answered, 'Not yet. I'm having a tough time with this fitting. Have a seat. I'll be out in a minute,' As I sat, the voice called back, 'Are you the *lone stranger?*' 'No,' I said. 'I'm Number One.' 'Don't leave,' he said, 'I'll be out before the cock crows three times.'

"After the minute passed, out from the back came a heavy-set woman, adjusting her tight garment. I figured it must have been the customer he was trying to fit. As she left the store, Moe came out, adjusting his zipper. 'I'm Moe, the tailor. How can I help? Vould you like to be fitted?' he said. 'No thanks,' I said, 'one minute. I must read my instructions.'

"Doing so, I said, 'I'm Number One. I was sent to pick up 12 full-length robes.' 'Yes,' said Moe, 'I have them ready. I understand they're to be vorn to a private supper party tomorrow evening.' 'Yes,' I said, 'I see that's what my instructions say.' 'May I ask, Number One,' said Moe, 'vat's your name?' Caught off guard, I said, 'Luigi.' 'That's no good,' said Moe. 'I'm thinking of taking on a partner. Moe and Luigi, it's not catchy enough. Vat's your last name?' Not wishing to divulge my true identity, I thought a moment and then said, 'Lord. Luigi Lord.' 'That's it!' said Moe. 'That's perfect. Ve'll call the shop, *Lord and Tailor*.' Thinking this guy must be *meshuggenah* (coocoo), I said, 'I must run. Good bye.'

"Once outside, I checked my instructions. Upon completion of business with the tailor, I proceeded to Vine and Branch Streets to make arrangements with the caterers. Entering, I met a gentleman. 'Hello, I'm Number One,' I said. 'I've been expecting you. I'm Eppes of Essence. Are you here to arrange for a private supper party?' 'Yes I am,' I said. 'Did you have anything special in mind?' he asked.

"Looking at my instructions, I said, 'It must be simple. I'll need a long table and thirteen chairs.' 'Thirteen!' said Eppes, 'Don't you know that's bad luck?' 'Don't worry,' I said. 'The word is out, some guy's leaving early.' 'All right already. Vat vould you like us to serve?' said Eppes.

"'According to instructions,' I said, 'start with chicken soup and matzo balls. For the appetizer, make it cream cheese and lox, ugh!' 'How about the entrée?' asked Eppes. Looking at the paper, I said, 'suckling pig.' Upset, Eppes said, 'Vait von minute here. Ve are a kosher house! Ve don't serve pigs!' 'In that case,' I said, 'I'll leave that up to you, as long as it's fresh.' 'Fresh!' said Eppes, 'Vat's the matter, do you doubt me?' I said, 'Not me, but I'm sure Thomas will, he doubts everybody! By the way, what kind of bread will you serve?' 'How's Jewish Rye?' asked Eppes. 'No, that's no good. The seeds get stuck in my choppers.' 'By the vay,' said Eppes, 'come by 5:00 p.m. and catch the early bird.' 'Thanks anyway but we can't. According to this letter, John's on lifeguard duty; some new recruits are getting their baptism underwater.' I said. 'Oh I see,' said Eppes. 'Vill this be the first time you've eaten here?' 'Yes,' I said, 'and more than likely my last. Shalom.'"

As Louie paused, Sonny asked, "Is that all, Uncle Louie?"

"No there's more. I still think it was that lox and cream cheese."

"What happened next?" asked Sonny.

"Let's see. Oh yes. It seems I'm seated at a long table with twelve other shmucks who all look alike."

"What do you mean?"

"Let me explain. We're all wearing matching white robes, brown sandals, black hair, and beards. No one is smiling, that is until some guy, also wearing a beard, walks in and says, 'My name is Lenny. I'm from Gotcha Pictures. I was asked to take a group portrait.' As he set up his camera and looked through the lens, he suddenly raised his head out from under the black cloth. Pointing at me, Lenny said, 'You, the guy on the end with the beady eyes, I'd like you to move to the middle. By the way, what's your name?' 'Number One,' I said. 'Jude, take his place on the end,' Lenny said.

"After switching places, he said, 'That's much better. O.K. everyone, say cheese!' He took the picture and then said, 'Perfect! The portrait will be ready in 30 minutes. Stop by my booth in the lobby.'

"Just as Lenny walked out the door, one of the twelve guys got up and left. As he did, Thomas said, 'Do you believe that guy?' Then I heard Paulie call out, 'Hey Jude, don't make it bad!' but by that time, he had already walked through the door. As he left, Eppes walked in.

"'Gentlemen,' he said, 'are any of you licensed fishermen?' Everyone raised their hands. 'Good,' said Eppes, 'you're all velcome to join us tomorrow. Ve're going out on a party boat sponsored by B'nai Brith.' Bart asked Eppes, 'So what are you fishing for?' 'Smoked vite fish,' said Eppes. That's when Pete said, 'Thanks, but tomorrow we're going on a fishing excursion in the Dead Sea.' Eppes said, 'Dead Sea! Holy Mackerel!' 'No' said Pete, 'soul!' 'Too bad,' said Eppes. 'Maybe you guys can make it to the Red Sea later. Some big shot, by the name of Moses is performing an aquatic extravaganza featuring *rolling stones*. Mazel tov.' And we raised our wine glasses in a toast.

"About then, Lenny the photographer walked in to announce the portraits were ready. 'By the way,' he said, 'if I failed to mention, my name's DaVinci, Leonardo DaVinci, but you can call me Lenny.' Suddenly Thomas, who doesn't trust a soul, stood up and said, 'I doubt that!'"

"You know something, Uncle Louie?" asked Sonny. "Why do I get the feeling you made the whole thing up? By the way, who is Number One?"

"My boy," said Louie, "it's part of the numbers game. It's for me to know and you to find out. Tell you what Sonny, some day when he comes back I'll personally introduce you to him."

"I realize it's a little early, but Jo wants to know if you'd like to spend a few days at our house during Easter week," said Sonny.

"Would I! You can count on me. I'll do anything to get away from all those bunnies," said Louie.

"Bunnies?" asked Sonny. "What bunnies?"

"Sometimes the auxiliary thinks we're 90-year-old kids. Oh, I know they mean well, but every damn holiday, they give each of us a bunch of stuffed animals. Until last year when I complained, there were so many in my room, I had no place to keep my sheep."

"Sheep? You mean to say they give you stuffed sheep too?" asked Sonny.

"No, not stuffed," said Louie, "real ones."

"Hold on a minute," said Sonny, "explain?"

"Because you took my book away, I began counting sheep, in order to fall asleep. But with all the damn stuffed bunnies in my room, there's no place for the poor sheep."

"So," said Sonny, "why don't you give some away?"

"Sheep?" asked Louie.

"No," said Sonny, "you know what I'm talking about."

Smiling Louie said, "Stuffed bunnies. I have a big problem. Dr. Feelfine told me to count sheep backwards, beginning with 99."

"Does it work?" asked Sonny.

"Like a charm. By the time I get to 79, I'm sound asleep."

"So what's the problem?" asked Sonny.

"When I wake to take a pee, I'm standing knee-deep in bunny pellets and sheep dip. Any chance you can come by and take some off my hands?" said Louie.

"Sure," said Sonny, "no problem. Wait 'til I run home and make room."

"Room?" asked Uncle Louie.

"That's right," said Sonny. "You see I fall asleep goosing butterflies."

As both began laughing, they bid one another good night.

Chapter 13
The Second Time Around

It was 12:30 Wednesday when Jo and Sonny arrived at Dumpsters to visit Louie. He wanted to introduce them to his new main squeeze, Mamie Cacciatore. The residents were in the dining room having lunch. In any facility that caters to the elderly, lunch is the heaviest meal of the day. With time on their hands, Sonny decided to give Jo a whirlwind tour of Dumpsters. Once that was over, they sat in the visitors' lounge, waiting for the couple.

At 1:30, residents began filing out of the dining room, heading in different directions. Aware that their visitors were waiting, Louie and Mamie went to the lounge. There they found Jo and Sonny sitting on the couch.

As they entered, Jo and Sonny stood to greet them. After the brief formality of introductions, they strolled onto the beautiful veranda, where they sat and began a very informative conversation.

It started with how happy they were to finally meet one another. Then Louie took hold of Mamie's hand and announced they were tying the knot. At first Sonny was caught off guard. After regaining his composure, he asked, "Have you set a date?"

"November 1st," said Mamie.

"Oh, how wonderful," said Jo. "I couldn't be happier for you both."

"If there is anything, anything either of us can do," said Sonny, "please let us know."

"To be honest," said Louie, "Mamie and I have been in the planning stages for several months. We wanted it to be a surprise. We joined the county-sponsored Planned Parenthood class. On Monday, we attended the first meeting."

Fighting to hold back his emotions, Sonny said, "Uncle Louie, what's the purpose of attending parenthood classes?"

He adamantly replied, "You never know, suppose the pill doesn't work and I get her in a family way!"

That did it. Jo and Sonny broke out into an explosion of hysterics. Laughter begets laughter, as the others joined in.

"What arrangements have been made to this point, Uncle Louie?"

"Our bridal party is nearly complete. Mamie's older sister, Concetta Frittata will be the matron of honor. My old buddy Guido Braciole—you remember my telling you about him; he's the retired undertaker—will be best man."

At that very instant, Herman, who happened to be passing, overhearing stopped dead in his tracks. "Sonny, did Louie tell you his old crony Braciole is hiring the ushers? Matter of fact, he's probably at the cemetery digging them up now as we speak."

"Ha ha!" said Louie. "Very funny, very funny indeed! You're a riot Short, or is that Shorty?"

"Just kidding Louie, just kidding. Don't get hot under the collar," he replied.

Mamie said, "Other than my sister Concetta and sister-in-law Casedia, all my relatives are gone."

"Would you like me to be a bridesmaid?" asked Jo.

"That won't be necessary," said Herman. "Braciole had a brilliant idea. He's getting them from 'Redi-Maid.' Not only that, but Louie's old buddy Guido is providing transportation absolutely free."

"That's fantastic," said Sonny. "Is the limo conventional or stretch?"

"Neither. It's a reconditioned hearse. He picked it up at a junkyard for a C-note," said Louie.

"Yes, but don't worry. By the time Guido gets done, it'll be like new. To tell the truth," said Herman, "that guy's so damn frugal, he made a deal with a gravedigger he knows. He's buying flowers from gravesites."

"There's only one thing missing," said Louie. "Mamie, you ask him."

"Sonny, would you do me the honor of giving the bride away?"

"Aunt Mamie, you don't mind if I call you Aunt Mamie, do you?"

"Not at all, nephew."

"I'm the one who'll be honored," said Sonny.

Beaming with joy, Mamie hugged Sonny and Jo.

Time seemed to fly, and before they knew it, the big day arrived. That morning, excitement radiated throughout Dumpsters. The entire staff was busy at work, helping prepare those residents in need. The manager of the beauty salon located on the premises brought in extra help to style hairdos. In Herman's words, "The joint was really jumpin'."

School buses donated to transport residents to church were waiting out front. Once everyone was on board, they pulled away, heading for their destination, the beautiful, brand-new Our Lady of Victory Church.

Shortly thereafter, the refurbished hearse pulled up. The bright November sun reflected off its highly-polished roof. Ms. Turnbuckle, the administrator, and her assistant, helped the loving couple into the back seat. Floral pieces, provided through the auspices of the dearly departed, filled the rear bed of the hearse, normally reserved for them. The happy couple was transported to the church.

Upon arrival, Louie got out and entered. Sonny was there to greet him. Herman was the ring bearer. The interior of the church was bursting at the seams. The aisles were filled with parked wheelchairs. The interior looked beautiful after the maintenance crew from Dumpsters strategically placed flowers on the altar.

The organist played as Sally Short sang the "Ave Maria." Everyone remained silent. Sally was not only a circus performer, but an accomplished chanteuse as well. Acknowledging the bridal party, the guests rose, when the organist played "The Wedding March."

At the altar, Louie's eyes became a little teary at the sight of his lovely bride-to-be. Guido grabbed hold of Louie's elbow and said, "Louie, you sure know how to pick 'em."

In the meantime, the procession moved down the white runner the ushers had rolled out. First came the matron of honor, Concetta Frittata, followed by the rest of the bridal party. Standing at the altar were Louie, Guido, and Father Richard, who patiently waited to perform the ceremony. It was very touching. After all, there are not many individuals their age still around, let alone getting married.

At the conclusion of the ceremony, the makeshift bridal party left the altar and made their way down the aisle toward the rear of the church. In the vestibule, guests went up to the reception line to offer best wishes. They exited to wait outside on the steps for the bridal party to leave the church. As they did, the guests roared with a vengeance. The happy couple was showered with rice, birdseed, crumbled crackers, an occasional banana and whatever else residents were able to confiscate at breakfast. Anyone who has worked in a nursing home or assisted-living facility is aware that some residents have a need to hoard food items beneath their clothing.

The newlyweds entered the hearse for the trip to the reception. For good luck, Sally Short threw a pair of old shoes. Later, Louie said, "Sally, it would have been better had you removed Herman from them!"

As wedding guests arrived at Dumpsters, they went directly to the recreation room. Volunteers, with the help of Philly and his maintenance crew, did a fantastic job decorating. The popular Barry, of "Barry Every Morning" fame donated the entertainment.

As the bridal party entered, a round of applause greeted them. Barry played the couple's favorite recording, "Smile," as they moved onto the dance floor. The bridal party and guests joined them.

Once everyone was seated, the best man Guido Braciole offered the toast. "Will everyone able please stand? Let's raise our glasses. Here's to you, Mr. and Mrs. Fettuccine.

'May you both outlive the redwoods,
May your lives be filled with joy.
Should you get your new bride pregnant,
We'll toast you once again, old boy.'"

Immediately thereafter, Father Richard blessed the meal. What a sumptuous respite the kitchen staff had prepared. Guests were offered a choice of three entrees: salt-free, sugar-free, and the always unpopular fat-free dinner.

After the main course, Mr. and Mrs. Fettuccine had their first piece of wedding cake. Feeding each other as is traditional, their faces were covered with cream. Barry, the entertainer, began the festivities with the garter throw. Louie got down on his arthritic knee. When Mamie raised her gown, Herman shouted, "Higher" while Louie removed it. He flung the garter, which landed on top of Herman's head.

Herman grabbed it, removed his jacket, and approached the fair lady. Under the watchful eye of Louie, he began to raise the garter up onto the new bride's limb. Pausing along the way, he turned to Louie and guests, rolled his eyes, and then smiled in Simon Legree fashion. Next came the ceremonial bridal bouquet toss. Ms. Turnbuckle was the recipient.

At the conclusion of the reception, the Fettuccines bid farewell, got into the hearse, and were whisked away to a nearby rendezvous in the heart of the Poconos, the Honeymoan Hotel. After checking in, the couple was shown to the bridal suite. Once in the room, Louie made a beeline for the bathroom. To his dismay, he was surprised to find the toilet bowl had no seat. Extremely upset, his bowels in an uproar, he called the manager.

"What kind of hotel is this? There's no seat on the crapper!"

"Sir, I'm sorry for the confusion, but I think you're referring to the *bidet*," replied the manager, who spoke with a French accent.

"The bi-what?"

"*Bidet*. It's for a woman's personal hygiene. You'll find the toilet behind a door in the *foyer*."

Louie slammed the phone down. "What did the manager say?" Mamie asked.

"I couldn't understand. He spoke with a thick French accent. This whole thing is driving me crazy. The object in that room is the *bi-day*, not the *toy-lay*. The toy-lay is in the *foy-yay*. All I know is I have to take a *shi-tay*."

While Louie was in the "whatchamacallit," Mamie proceeded to empty their suitcases. In doing so, she realized she neglected to pack her baby dolls, and became upset.

When Louie came out of the bathroom, he found his new bride sitting on the edge of the bed, sobbing. "What happened? Did you hurt yourself?"

Weeping louder, she said, "No!"

"Are you sorry we got married?"

"No!" she said, gasping for breath.

"Well then, what the hell's the matter?"

"I…I forgot my baby dolls."

"Holy cow. Do you still play with those damn things?"

"No. I'm talking about my sexy pajamas."

"Oh," said Louie. "So what? I forgot my BVDs, but you don't see me bawling! At least not yet! Come on Mamie," he continued. Putting his arm around her shoulder he tried to comfort her. "Let's go to bed. It's after 8 p.m."

Exhausted from their trying day, the two lovebirds snuggled under the covers and fell asleep. Not long after a knocking on the door awakened them. They heard a voice calling, "Fern, Fern, let me in."

Angered, Louie shouted, "Stop banging on my door." Looking at the clock, he noticed it was 8:45. "Can't you see what time it is? There's no damn Fern in here!"

"Oh, be quiet, you old fart," said the man. "I'm not knocking on your door. I'm trying to awaken my boyfriend." The Honeymoan catered to both straight and gay seniors.

Next thing they heard was the opening and closing of a door across the hall. Once again silence fell, as the newlyweds went back to sleep.

Around 10 p.m., he got up for the first of four visits to relieve himself. Climbing back into bed, he heard voices next door. Mamie awakened, as the voices grew louder. Sitting up in bed, they heard, through the paper-thin walls of the adjoining room, an old geezer (as Louie referred to old men) moaning, "I wish I could, I wish I might, I wish I could do something tonight."

Soon followed by his partner's response, "I wish you could, I wish you might, shit or get off the pot tonight!"

The back-and-forth exchange continued for three hours, until a calm settled in.

The following morning, between peeing and listening to the moaning next door, the newlyweds were exhausted. They decided to have breakfast in bed. Mamie had an order of stewed prunes and a bowl of farina sprinkled with wheat germ. Louie had a tall glass of prune juice spiked with fiber and a side of mushy bananas. "I hate anything soft," said Louie.

Smiling, Mamie said, "Me too!"

After breakfast, they relaxed to digest their food. Now came time to take their medication. Between the both of them, they swallowed over 30 pills. Mamie entered the bathroom to put on her red string bikini. Louie, in turn, put on his old-fashioned wool bathing suit. Once suited, they got into the Jacuzzi.

"Woman, you're hot!" Louie said.

The remainder of Louie's day was filled with various activities: shuffleboard, bingo, and occasional attempts at dipping into the honey pot.

Due to a computer glitch, several young women attending a strippers' convention at another Pocono resort inadvertently ended up at the Honeymoan.

Sunday morning, Mamie and Louie attended early Mass in the chapel. With spirits rejuvenated, they stopped by to enjoy the champagne brunch being offered by the hotel.

Returning to their room, they decided to don swimsuits, heading down to the lakeside beach for a little sun and relaxation. About an hour or so passed when Mamie said, "Louie, I feel a bit chilly. I'm going to the room to get my sweater. I'll be right back."

"O.K., my dear, I think I'll take a little nap," said Louie.

Not long after Mamie left, Louie felt a gentle tug on his shoulder. As he opened his eyes, sitting on a blanket beside him, was a young, voluptuous blonde. The sweet young thing asked, "Sir, sorry to bother you, but I was wondering if you'd do me a favor."

Recognizing her to be one of the female strippers staying at the hotel, Louie said, "Certainly. It's no bother at all." Fumbling for words, he continued, "What would you like me to do to you? I mean, *for* you?"

Giggling at the elderly man's confusion, she said, "Would you mind spreading this sunscreen on my back?"

Gulping, he said, "Mind? I don't mind at all. The pleasure would be all mine."

"Thank you, sir." Then she rolled over and lowered her bra strap as she flopped down. Because she was well endowed, the pressure forced her breasts to extend out to the sides of her upper torso.

Louie's beady eyes opened wide to envelop the full view presented before him. Falling to his knees, he hastily unscrewed the cap from the tube, squeezing a small portion onto his hands. "Are you ready?"

"Yes," the damsel answered as she raised her head. Swishing her long blond hair, exposing her beautiful face, she gave Louie a sensual smile.

Aroused, he began applying sunscreen. As his hands circled her velvety-smooth back, his fingers somehow managed to touch the outer edges of her bosom, causing her to sigh with pleasure.

"You have such wonderful hands," she said. "I'm going to roll over so you can do my front. Hope you don't mind?"

Louie blushed like a schoolboy. While applying additional lotion to his hands, the sweet young thing rolled over. Just then, Louie heard a familiar voice.

"Mr. Fettuccine! May I ask what you think you're doing?" said Mamie.

Opening his eyes, Louie said, "What are you talking about?"

"You're moaning like a young man having his first sexual encounter, she said. Not only that, your chest is completely covered with sun lotion. Everyone's looking at you. What's going on?"

Sitting up, thinking quickly, he said, "I fell asleep and was dreaming of you."

"My, oh my," said Mamie, "would you like to go up to the room, my love?"

"That's a good idea," he said. "I think I've got to go. I'll be right back."

Later that afternoon, Louie complained about the sunburn he'd gotten, especially the burn on his face. Looking in the mirror, he said, "Well, I'll be. You know something? Even my tongue's burned."

"It's little wonder," replied Mamie, "the way you were wagging your tongue like a dog in heat."

Friday morning, after checkout, Louie spoke to the manager, telling him the walls were too thin. "They're so damn thin, you can hear every little fart," he said. "Another thing: Do yourself a favor and change the name of the hotel from Honeymoan to *Torrid Zone*."

"How's that?" asked the manager.

Cupping his hand to his mouth, he said, "You can meet some pretty hot numbers here. When I was a youngster and mentioned sex, some smart-ass broad would say, 'In your dreams.' Until I came here I never realized how right she was!"

With a gleam in his eye, and a spring in his gait, he left to find Mamie patiently waiting in the hearse.

Chapter 14
All about Mamie

The honeymoon was over. Left with sweet memories, the newlyweds were chauffeured back to Dumpsters. Louie and Mamie entered into an interesting conversation regarding her first marriage.

Louie said, "Tell me, Mamie, what was your first husband like?"

"Joe was extremely possessive," she said. "He was also very well off."

"How's that?" asked Louie.

"He was connected," she said, "if you know what I mean."

"You're talking mob connected?" Louie said.

"That's right, Louie. Have you heard of Joseph Cacciatore?"

"You mean *Chicken Joe?* Sure have," said Louie. "Who hasn't heard of *Chicken Cacciatore*? How did you hook up with a bird like that?"

"I was young and foolish. I was born in New York's Little Italy. A girlfriend of mine introduced me to Joe, thinking she was doing me a favor. At the time we met, I was only 16. It was during a neighborhood party following *La Festa il Santo Gennaro* held yearly in Little Italy. Struck by his good looks and sweet talk, I fell madly in love. Not realizing what I was letting myself in for, I married, later regretting that unfortunate decision.

"He was indicted on charges of corruption," she said. "In order to save his hide, he informed on other mob members. When they found out he ratted on them, he was executed gangland style."

"Yes," said Louie, "I recall reading about it in the newspapers. I can still see the headline, 'Authorities Believe Fowl Play Led to the Killing of Gangland's Tough Old Bird, Chicken Joe.' The article read something like this: 'Plucked from the icy waters of the Hudson, Joe's gullet was slit and both his wings broken. Cacciatore was burned beyond recognition.'

"Mamie, it was scum like him that defamed Italians. People should focus on the true Italians who gave so much to the world; like Michelangelo, DaVinci, Galileo, Vespucci, Columbus, and Marconi. During WW II, American boys of Italian descent formed the largest ethnic group, helping to win the war."

Mamie nodded in agreement.

"I guess he left you pretty well off," said Louie.

"Not at all," answered Mamie. "The government confiscated whatever money was left, as payment for tax evasion."

"What did you do? How did you live?" Louie asked.

"Like any other woman in a similar situation. I pulled myself up by my bootstraps, left New York for New Jersey, and settled in a small apartment in the borough of Roseland. It was made possible by meager savings I managed to accumulate over the years. I found a job in the town's finance department. At the end of 20 years, I retired. Within six months, boredom set in, so I decided to attend Vale Business School for Realtors. After graduation, I took the New Jersey real estate exam, passed, and received my Realtor's license. I was employed by the Wayward Agency, later becoming manager."

"I knew you were a smart cookie, Mamie," Louie said. "Go on."

"One very warm July day, as I sat doing listings, the phone rang. I said, 'Good morning, Wayward Realty, Mamie Cacciatore speaking. May I help you?'

"At the other end I heard a voice answer in a thick foreign accent. 'This is Patudy. Ve vant buy house. You can do these ting? My vife, Upu, come vit me, hokay?' 'Certainly Mr. Patudy,' I said. 'When may I expect you?' 'Ve be there right vay, you vait,' he said.

"At first I thought it might have been one of the guys in our office playing a prank, so I paid no thought. About 15 minutes later, my doubts were laid to rest as the front door swung open and in walked the odd couple."

"What made them odd?" asked Louie.

"Well," said Mamie, "Mr. Patudy stood 6'10", thin as a beanpole. His wife was 5'5", probably weighing somewhere in the neighborhood of 300 pounds.

"'Hi lo,' said Mr. Patudy. 'My name's Maash Patudy, my vife, Upu Patudy. You voman I talk to?' he asked. 'Ve vant house. You show?' 'Yes Mr. Patudy, please sit down so I can qualify you. I must find your price range,' I said. 'No vorry 'bout price,' he said, 'Patudy have much duel-r. You tell price.'

"Looking through my listings earlier, I noticed a new house priced in the mid-$100s came on the market. Trying to get a handle on his range, I showed him a picture of the house, telling him it was listed for $170,000. As I started to ask if they would like to inspect the house, he pulled out two fists full of $1,000 bills. 'I buy,' he said, 'you show.' 'All right,' I said, 'first

I need some personal information.' Upon completion of the forms, I showed the couple to my car and taxied them to the house."

"Were they able to afford it?" Louie asked.

"Able to, you ask?" said Mamie. "Louie, they were loaded. There was one thing that bothered me."

"What was that?" asked Louie.

"From the minute they walked in the front door, 'til the time we arrived at the house, Mrs. Patudy never uttered a sound."

"That's a bit strange," Louie said.

"Not only that, but because she expressed no emotions, I was unable to get a read on her. I was astonished by the fact that in mid-July, with afternoon temperatures climbing into the nineties, she wore a fur coat."

"She must have been a real cracker jack," said Louie.

"The three of us got out of the car and entered the house," said Mamie.

"Once inside, Mr. Patudy said, 'I like, I take!' 'Mr. Patudy,' I said, 'before making a rash decision, let me show you the rest of the house.' 'Okey dokey,' he said. 'Upu come, ve look.' As we turned, she was nowhere to be seen. 'Ver the hell she go?' he asked. 'I haven't the slightest idea,' I said. Then I called 'Mrs. Patudy, Mrs. Patudy, where are you?' 'Upu, ver you go?' he yelled.

"Suddenly coming from upstairs, we heard sounds similar to what a trapped animal might make. As we made our way up the staircase, they seemed to be coming from the master suite. We entered the bedroom, and then walked into the bathroom. Lo and behold, sprawled in the tub was Mrs. Patudy. Still wrapped in fur, she looked like a polar bear, struggling to free herself."

"My gosh, I can't believe what I'm hearing," Louie said. "I'll bet Mr. Patudy was upset."

"That's putting it mildly. He said, 'Vat you do, you crazy voman?' To my surprise, she said, 'I vant see if tub fit. I get stuck!' Furious, Mr. Patudy said, 'You see if toilet fit too? Come, I help you out. You make me craz.' Turning to me, he said, 'You know this thirty house ve see.' He eyed is wife and said, 'Upu, you big ass no fit in toilet bowl, either. You vill get stuck all the time.' He then looked at me and said, 'Sorry Missus, ve no buy house today. You take back please?' Once he helped his wife from the tub, we got into my car and drove back. After arriving at the office, we said our good-byes and they left."

Louie asked, "What happened after that?"

"I quit real estate," said Mamie, "and took early retirement."

When the honeymooners arrived, standing in front of Dumpsters was Ms. Turnbuckle and a few of her staff. The outpouring of affection showered upon the newlyweds caused the couple to break down.

"Come now," said Ms. Turnbuckle, "we'll have none of that. This is a joyous occasion! Follow me, we have a surprise waiting."

Entering the building, the newlyweds were led down the hallway to a recently constructed wing of Dumpsters.

"Wait here a minute," said Ms. Turnbuckle. Walking several steps ahead, she opened a door. "Please close your eyes and don't open 'til I tell you." Following Ms. Turnbuckle's instructions, she led the newlyweds into the room. "Open your eyes," she said.

They looked around and were astounded by what they saw. The room had to be at least 30 by 30. In the center was a beautiful king-size poster bed covered with a white silk comforter. In front of the large picture window stood two leather swivel chairs. To the side was a TV screen. The floor covering was a plush rose-colored broadloom. The bathroom contained a double sink, shower, and bathtub. It was magnificent. Awestruck, the newlyweds didn't utter a word.

"Well Mr. and Mrs. Fettuccine, what do you think?" said Ms. Turnbuckle.

With tear-filled eyes, Mamie said, "What can we say? We're delighted!" She walked over and gave Ms. Turnbuckle a hug.

Louie said, "There's just one thing I'd like to know. Is this covered under Medicare?"

Winking, Ms. Turnbuckle said, "Absolutely."

"By the way," said Louie. "Before we move in, we must have Mamie's dear friend, Upu Patudy, try out the tub."

Mamie looked at Louie, smiling.

"Just kidding," he said. "It's an inside joke."

"Let's take a walk over to the recreation room," said Ms. Turnbuckle. "There's something I'd like you to see."

Back down the corridor they made their way to the recreation room. As Ms. Turnbuckle opened the door, shouts of "Surprise! Surprise!" filled the air. One of the volunteers from the women's auxiliary played the couple's favorite song, "Smile." Once again, tears filled their eyes, as they were encouraged to dance. The residents and staff sang. The newlyweds obliged and began dancing. As they moved across the floor, they noticed the smiling faces of Big Bertha, Sally, Herman, Ms. Turnbuckle, Guido Braciole, and of course, Jo and Sonny. The residents and guests helped themselves to the buffet prepared by Big Sam and his kitchen staff. The party broke up around 10:00 p.m. In a corner of the room, Mamie and Louie remained, talking with Jo, Sally, Herman, and Sonny.

"I can't get over it," said Mamie. "How can we ever show our gratitude to all those responsible for tonight?"

"Yes," said Louie, "everything's wonderful. To be honest, Mamie and I are a little bushed. It's been an exhausting but glorious day."

After exchanging farewells, everyone called it a night.

The following day, around ten, Sonny's phone rang.

"Hi Sonny, this is Aunt Mamie. Did you guys enjoy yourselves last night?"

"We sure did. It was one heck of a party. Is Uncle Louie up yet?"

"Yes," said Mamie, "he just walked over to meet his cronies to play a few hands of poker. The reason I'm calling is to speak to Jo. Is she available?"

"Sure," said Sonny. "Please hold. I'll get her to the phone." Holding the receiver off to the side, he called out, "Jo, Jo, it's for you!"

"Who is it?" asked Jo.

"Aunt Mamie," said Sonny. "She wants to speak with you."

"O.K., ask her to hold on. I'll pick up down here," said Jo. "Hello, Aunt Mamie. How are you feeling after last night?"

"Great, Jo," said Aunt Mamie. "I'd like to discuss something with you."

"Hold one minute," said Jo.

Cupping the mouthpiece, she turned to Sonny to ask where he was going.

"Just down to the store. I want to pick up some O.J. and milk," said Sonny.

"Sorry, Aunt Mamie," said Jo. "What's up?"

While Sonny was out, he decided to stop at the hardware store to pick up a trap. Somehow or other, a flying squirrel got into the house. A good hour had passed since he left. After finishing his chores, he returned to find Jo still gabbing on the phone. In the meantime, he got out a jar of peanut butter, placed some on the trap and set it, trying to catch the flying squirrel. As he put it in place, Jo walked into the kitchen.

"What was that about?" Sonny asked.

"Aunt Mamie called to find out if we'd like to take a trip to Hawaii with them," said Jo.

"What did you tell her?" asked Sonny.

"I wanted to get your reaction first," said Jo.

"I think it would be fun; let's do it," said Sonny. "Call back for particulars."

Jo picked up the phone and began dialing. "Did you set the trap?" asked Jo. "Oh hello Aunt Mamie, it's Jo calling back."

"Yes Jo, what does Sonny think?"

"He thought it would be fun. Do you have any information?" asked Jo.

"No that's what I wanted to talk about," said Mamie. "Any chance you could pick us up and take us to the travel agency?"

"Hold a minute," Jo said, turning away from the receiver she yelled to Sonny, "Aunt Mamie wants to know when would be a good time to visit the travel agent and book our trip."

Calling down, Sonny said, "Tell her tomorrow at 10:00 a.m."

"Aunt Mamie we'll pick you up at 10:00 a.m. sharp."

"Fine," she said, "we'll be waiting."

"Good-bye, see you then," said Jo as she hung up.

Bright and early the following morning, the newlyweds dressed, had breakfast, and waited outside. Sonny and Jo came on time. After picking them up, they headed for the travel agency, while there they made arrangements for their trip. The itinerary specified they'd fly out of Newark December 10th for a two-week stay in Hawaii. The flight was scheduled for 12:40 p.m. A limo was to pick them up at 9:20 a.m. In order to expedite matters, Sonny and Jo had the couple stay overnight.

That evening, a significant snowfall had been predicted. Playing safe, Sonny asked his son-in-law Anthony to plow the driveway. He was the kind of kid, no matter what Sonny asked, he could always be counted on to help. Overnight, the white stuff piled up significantly.

Early in the morning, Anthony and his six-year-old son, Mark, were on the job, clearing the way for the limo. Due to road conditions, the driver arrived a few minutes early. It was a good thing he did. Route 80 in Pennsylvania had outgrown its usefulness. As expected, it was slow going 'til they got to New Jersey. At Newark International, they left the limo and checked in. It was a long wait, but they were patient. Their flight departed on schedule; destination, Los Angeles International Airport. After touchdown, the pilot informed passengers that due to technical problems, there would be a three-hour layover and change of aircraft.

"Oh well," Sonny said, "let's make the best of it."

"I guess that's all we can do," said Jo.

After leaving the plane, the four travelers found a quiet corner and sat down. To pass time, they picked up some magazines and snacks. Poor Louie, his kidneys were working overtime. Excusing himself, he made his third trip to the men's room. Only this time, he didn't return, not that any of the group noticed, for they had fallen asleep. Sometime later, Louie returned to explain what had taken place.

"Quick," he said, "wake up. They're shooting an episode of *Jack and the Thin Man*. Guess what, we're all going to be in it."

"Are you pulling my leg again?" asked Sonny.

"No, I swear I'm telling the truth. When I came from the men's room, instead of walking back this way, I became disoriented and walked in the opposite direction. This terminal all looks alike. Then I noticed a great deal of commotion going on in a far-off corner.

"As I approached, a gentleman wearing glasses, carrying a megaphone waved me over. In a high-pitched voice, he asked if I was one of the extras. Upon closer inspection, I noticed a TV cameraman and the stars of the series. Stumbling for words, I said, 'Yes I am.' 'Were you sent over from casting?' he asked. Again I answered, 'Yes.' 'Where the hell are the others?' he asked. 'Have you seen them?' Without hesitation I said, 'Of course.' 'Would you mind getting them?' he asked. 'Tell them we're shooting in 25 minutes.' 'Sure, I'll get them pronto,' I said. So here I am. Now come on, don't waste time. Let's make tracks. We're going to become TV stars!"

Putting on their coats and hats, they gathered their luggage, which they were told to take with them due to the change of aircraft, and followed Louie.

Spotting them, the rotund bespectacled man said to Louie, "Thank God you found them. Hurry, there's no time to lose; we're ready to shoot."

Sonny thought 'Here's the four of us dressed in winter clothes dragging our suitcases, while the stars and other extras were dressed in tropical wear.'

"Listen up people," shouted the director. "Here's the plot. As you folks…" (pointing to the four of them) "…stand in line at the check-in counter, Jack will be talking to the agent. Suddenly a terrorist will approach from behind and place a gun to Jack's temple. You, you with the beady eyes!"

Louie said, "Me? Are you talking to me?"

"Yes," the director said, "what's your name?"

"Fettuccine, Louie Fettuccine," he said.

"Louie," he said, "I want you and your group at the head of the line."

They were told to approach the counter just prior to the star's appearance, get their boarding passes, and then walk away. It felt as though it was close to 90 degrees in that section of the terminal. What with the spotlights and all, they began perspiring freely.

"Any questions?" asked the director. "If not, consider this a go. Ready, camera, action."

Louie moved out first. Somehow, during baggage transfer, they failed to secure the lock properly. As luck would have it the suitcase opened and the contents, including his enema bag, spilled on the floor.

In disgust, the director yelled, "Cut!" as some of the crew ran to help replace the contents into the suitcase. Embarrassed, Louie returned to the line.

After approximately 20 takes, the director said, "That's a wrap."

As far as the four were concerned, it came none too soon. Lugging those suitcases back and forth dressed in overcoats was a bit much.

Just then a voice on the loudspeaker announced, "All passengers traveling from Los Angeles to Hawaii, return to Gate 10, we'll be boarding in 20 minutes."

Completely exhausted, Sonny spotted a transportation cart. After explaining their dilemma, the attendant agreed to help and they started loading their bags. The project's payroll clerk walked over. She explained extras are entitled to be paid. Louie asked, "How much?"

"Five dollars per hour," she said, "we owe you 10 dollars each."

With no time to waste, boarding the cart, Louie said, "Miss, donate our earnings to Actor's Equity. You never know when we might need it."

Off they hurried to catch their flight. Once on board, they found their seats, buckled up, and began reminiscing about their acting careers. Not long after the aircraft was airborne, the flight attendants began passing out meals. With bellies full, they closed their eyes as the 747 headed to their destination.

As Louie fell asleep, he began to dream. Seated next to him, he imagined, was the director he'd just worked with. Shaking his hand the director said, "You're the guy with the beady eyes. What did you say your name was?" "Fettuccine," Louie said. "Perfect! You'd be perfect for the war drama I'm shooting," he said. "What part do I play?" Louie asked. "The pharmacist," he said. "You're sure you don't mean medic?" Louie questioned.

Louie continued, "What's the title of this war drama anyway?" "*From Here to the Pharmacy*," the director answered. "You play the part of a drug dealer. Your name is Maggio Gelato. The scene opens with you standing behind the counter, concocting a milkshake. The door opens and in walks Fatso, a sadistic Head Sergeant." "Are you sure you don't mean Top Sergeant?" Louie asked. "No, he's the Head Sergeant. He's in charge of latrines," he said. "Because of inner thigh chafing, he's in excruciating pain. He enters the store and angrily says, *'If my salve isn't ready, I'm going to splatter you all over the wall!'*" "I'll kill that S.O.B.!" Louie shouted. The director had a gleam in his eye and said, "Good, good, that's the spirit; I knew you'd be perfect for the part. Save your anger for the shoot."

The director continued, "Fatso is extremely upset; working latrine duty has given him a piss-poor attitude. You walk from behind the counter, hand him his salve, telling him he owes 50 bucks. Then say your lines, *'Look Fatso, you wouldn't have prickly heat if you'd keep out of the cat house.'* Then you and he head for the alley to act out the fight scene. Be sure to overemphasize your bowlegged walk," said the director, whose name was Willie B. Ware. "I don't get it," said Louie. "What does my being bowlegged have to do with a war drama?" "Nothing," he said, "but your walk and your next line are what make the scene work. You say, *'Walk this way, Fatso!'* In pain, he shouts, *'Damn you, Gelato. If I could walk that way, I wouldn't have to spend 50 bucks for this cream!'*"

Having slept the entire way, Louie suddenly awakened in response to a boom followed by passengers screaming. At first, he thought the attack on Pearl Harbor had begun. Opening his eyes, he noticed everyone panicking. Once awake, he too began to panic. What actually happened was, when the plane hit the tarmac, wind shear caught the nose, elevating it to a 45-degree angle before falling back to earth.

After taxiing to the ramp, they disembarked the aircraft. Unable to locate the director, Louie realized it was just another dream.

Sonny cupped his hand to his mouth and said, "You know, Uncle Louie, to be honest, back there I nearly shit my pants."

"To be honest with you, Sonny," Louie said, "I did. Where the hell's the latrine? I have to get rid of this underwear. It's beginning to run down my leg."

Louie hurried to the men's room, praying he wouldn't run into Fatso. Luckily there was an infant's changing station. He disposed of his soiled underwear, washed and then helped himself to several diapers. When he returned, standing with the others was the tour guide. After getting their bags, they walked to a waiting limo. Two Hawaiian beauties greeted them, giving each a lei. He didn't know about Sonny, but it was the first time in years a young woman had given him one.

Once inside the limo, they were transported to their destination, the Mala-ook-ya Suites. Their corner rooms offered a sweep-around balcony, affording views of both ocean and mountains.

That first evening was one they would always remember. At the luau, roasted pig and other tropical delicacies were served.

Louie told the others, "I don't know about you, but this pig tastes almost as good as Big Sam's ham hocks."

The following morning at breakfast, they met a very interesting Japanese couple. During World War II, he served in the Imperial Japanese Army. Almost ashamed of what his government had done, he said, "Japan may not have won the Hawaiian islands during the war, but somehow, the Japanese ended up owning all the businesses." The stories he told made the hair on the back of their necks stand up. Humbly, again he apologized for the sneak attack on Pearl Harbor.

That afternoon, they took a navy launch to the Arizona Memorial. It was sad indeed to think that below lay so many young, innocent Americans. Returning to the hotel, they went back to their rooms.

Once inside, Louie asked Mamie, "What's that noxious odor?"

"I don't know," she said, "but it's awful."

"Let's get out of here," Louie said. "Wait in the hall; I'll get Sonny." After explaining what happened, Sonny accompanied Louie back to his room. Opening the door, he said, "Good grief! Who died and was buried here?"

Rushing into the hallway, he picked up the house phone and called security. When they arrived, they too were overcome by the stench. Without further delay, security called for the plumber and hotel manager to come immediately. Within minutes, they arrived. The two men entered the room. The manager came running out gasping for air, while the poor plumber remained.

White under the gills, the manager said, "Please accept my apologies. I can't explain how it happened; it seems the plumbing backed into the tub. There is no need for further discussion. I'm upgrading you to one of our penthouse suites. I'll have your bags transferred immediately. I'm so sorry."

From the tone of his voice, Louie knew he was in the driver's seat.

"Wait," he said. "What about my nephew and his wife? We must have rooms close by."

"Of course, that's a given. They can have the adjoining penthouse," he said. "I'd also like you to have breakfast on me."

"Would that be for the remainder of our stay?" Louie asked.

Without a whimper he said, "Mr. Fettuccine. I wouldn't have it any other way."

Later, Sonny asked, "Uncle Louie, how did you pull that off?"

Louie said, "My boy, my father told me a long time ago, when you've got them dead to rights, play your strongest suit. I knew I had him by the short hairs, so I struck while the iron was hot. If I ever run across the guy who dumped that load in the tub, I'll kiss him."

As they spoke, the doorbell rang. The bellhops brought in their luggage, and carts filled with champagne, fresh fruits, cheeses, crackers, and chocolates.

When they left, Louie said, "See Sonny, we've hit the mother lode!"

Kidding, Sonny said, "I thought you said the load belonged to some guy."

"Whatever," Louie said, "we pulled off a major coup."

The next week and a half was spent living in the lap of luxury. They paid visits to the usual tourist attractions. None impressed them more than their visit to Pearl Harbor. On the final day, they boarded their plane for the return flight to the mainland.

As the aircraft circled over the Arizona Memorial, Louie said to Mamie, "You may rest assured those brave souls would *never say uncle*."

"Yes," said Mamie, "I have to agree."

Chapter 15
Clear Case of Discrimination

The other morning, while having breakfast, Jo and Sonny sat watching *Good Morning America*. The network was airing a special presentation originating from Washington D.C.

At the program's conclusion, Sonny said, "Seeing pictures of our nation's capital stirred up a long-time desire to visit there."

"Me too!" said Jo.

"That settles it," said Sonny. Lifting the receiver, he rang Dumpsters, asking to be connected to his uncle's room. During their conversation, Sonny explained of his plan to visit the capital next week. Louie told him the timing was perfect, because Herman asked him to help with his discrimination suit. At the conclusion of their conversation, Sonny told Louie he would see him when he returned. Two weeks later, Sonny went to visit Louie.

"Hi Sonny," said Louie. "How is President George W. feeling? You have to hand it to Mr. Bush; he's not one to take guff from anybody. Reminds me of his predecessor, Ronald Reagan."

"I'll second that," said Sonny. "Both he and Rudy Giuliani deserve credit for calming our fears following the terrorist attack on 9/11."

"God bless them and all who serve to protect America's freedom," said Louie.

"What's this you're telling me about Herman starting a discrimination suit?" asked Sonny.

"Herman's my best friend. I love him dearly, but when the little guy goes off on a tangent, there's no changing his mind," said Louie. "It all began when the county commissioners issued a statement designating the week of August 5th Employ Older Workers Week. Herman told me he read an ad in the newspaper's help wanted section advertising for lifeguard duty. Herman checked it out. Two weeks after doing so, he received a letter from them stating he failed to meet the requirements."

"What was the name of the organization?" asked Sonny.

"WHY!" said Louie.

"No special reason," said Sonny, "just asking."

"That's the name," said Louie, "W-H-Y, it stands for We Help Youth."

"Oh, I see," said Sonny, "tell more."

"Herman was upset. He decided to hire one of the oldest law firms in the Poconos: Castrovitabellanote and Castrovitabellanote."

Sonny asked, "Uncle Louie, isn't that the name of one of the residents?"

"Yes," said Louie, "He's a retired attorney."

"I thought you told me he was ill," said Sonny.

"I did. Herman had no choice but to hire him."

"Why is that?" asked Sonny.

"His fees were very attractive," Louie said. "He did it for nothing."

"On what grounds did Herman base his case?" asked Sonny.

"Age and promptness," said Louie.

"Would you mind explaining?"

"Not at all. Two weeks ago Herman was responding to the ad. He arrived before the appointed time of 8:00 a.m. on Tuesday the 15th."

"What time did the other applicants arrive?" asked Sonny.

"8:00 a.m. sharp," said Louie "Herman felt that was the first infraction."

"I'm confused. How long before was Herman there?"

"Ten minutes," said Louie.

"Ten minutes before eight?" Sonny asked.

"No! Before six," Louie said.

"If I understand correctly," said Sonny, "you're telling me Herman arrived two hours and ten minutes before eight on Tuesday?"

"No!" said Louie, "two hours and ten minutes before eight on *Monday.*"

"Wait a minute," said Sonny, "I was under the impression Herman's interview was scheduled 8:00 a.m. Tuesday."

"It was," said Louie. "Herman's a stickler for being on time. His motto is 'early to rise, early to eat.' Seniors are always someplace long before they should be. They practically pound the doors down to get them open."

"Did he have the interview?"

"Herman said that's when the second problem occurred. He felt due to his age, the interviewer asked him a lot of questions that had nothing to do with the job," said Louie.

Sonny asked, "What took place during the interview?"

"The questioning went like this: When asked to state his full name Herman answered, 'Short, Herman Short.' Then he was asked his age; '86-plus' was his answer. Next he was asked if he had Red Cross training and Herman answered, 'No just *Blue*.' 'How long can you stay afloat?' was the next question. Herman said, 'That depends!' 'On what?' said the interviewer. 'Whether or not I had a bowel movement,' said Herman. 'In the event of drowning what would you do?' asked the interviewer. 'I'd yell like hell, HELP! HELP!' The interviewer said, 'No, no! I don't mean you, I mean if someone else was drowning.' 'Oh,' said Herman. 'In that case I'd pray.' 'Pray!' said the interviewer, 'Pray for what?' 'Pray for someone to save the poor bastard from drowning,' Herman said. The interviewer said, 'Sir that's what the job you're applying for requires you to do.' 'Wait a minute, buddy, you've got to be kidding, I can't swim a stroke.' said Herman."

"Then why did he apply for the job?" asked Sonny.

"That's exactly what the interviewer wanted to know," said Louie. "The interviewer said, 'You can't? Then why did you apply for lifeguard duty?' Herman said, 'Lifeguard duty? I thought the ad said light guard duty.' The interviewer said, 'Mr. Short I think I've heard quite enough. That concludes our interview. You'll hear from us in about two weeks. Watch your mail.'

"Two weeks later, after receiving his response, he decided to prosecute the W-H-Y," said Louie. "When the case was thrown out of court, Herman fired Castrovitabellanote."

"Why?" asked Sonny.

Louie said, "Herman told me he felt Castrovitabellanote was sick, and had *ill* advised him."

"Is Herman still pursuing the case?" asked Sonny.

"Yes," said Louie, "He's going the public defender route."

"Who's been assigned to his case?" asked Sonny.

"Some little crackpot by the name of Herman Short," said Louie. "Enough of this craziness, I have something important to tell you. We're having a *Senior Prom.*"

"Really," said Sonny, "that's wonderful. You're not kidding, are you?"

"No way! Don't take my word, here comes the *Attorney General,* ask him. "Herman, tell my nephew where we're going next Friday night," said Louie.

"Oh you mean the Senior Prom," said Herman.

"See, I told you, Sonny," said Louie. "I wasn't kidding."

"Well, in that case, tell me all about it," said Sonny.

"Last week," said Louie, "students from Swiftwater Elementary School dropped by for the annual sing-along. It's wonderful to think young folks take time from their burdensome schedules to entertain us."

"I'll say," said Sonny. "I think that's the trend since September 11th. President Bush's call for volunteerism has touched all Americans."

"Louie, tell Sonny about the Senior Prom," said Herman.

"Hold on, will you? That's what I'm about to do. As I started to say, a group of kids thought up the idea. Actually it's a prom for seniors. It's a formal affair. The guys are going to the mall to get fitted for their tuxes. The girls are there trying on gowns as we speak."

"Can you believe it?" asked Herman. "Local service clubs joined together with the business community to foot the bill."

"Wow," said Sonny, "that's wonderful."

"That's only the half of it. They've rented a beautiful facility to hold it at. Red Herring's Pennsylvanians were hired to play," said Louie.

"I understand they had trouble digging them up," said Herman.

"The theme will be 'Never Say Uncle,'" said Louie. "That's not all. Friday evening, a fleet of limos has been hired to transport us to the prom. A special menu, catering to dietary needs, is being served. Dumpsters' resident dietician has been instrumental in preparing the menu."

Sonny asked, "Will you be eating the food she recommends?"

"Who me?" he said. "I'll be damned if I'm going to eat like a scared rabbit. I'm putting on the old feed bag."

"That goes for me too," said Herman. "After the prom, we're heading down the shore to get a little nookie. Hot damn! Isn't that the cat's meow?"

"Dream on," said Louie. "If we're still alive after what's planned, come Saturday morning, we'll be too pooped to poop."

Sonny said, "I suppose I'll have to wait 'til next week to learn the outcome. See you then."

Sonny could hardly wait to get home to tell Jo. He knew when he did, she'd get a kick out of it. After arriving home, he found a note saying she'd gone to the store to pick up a few items. Not more than ten minutes passed when the phone rang. It was Louie calling.

"Hi Sonny," he said, "Sorry to bother you. I forgot to show you the letter I received in the mail. I need a bit of advice. Do you mind if I read it to you?" he said.

"Not at all. What's it about?" asked Sonny.

"It's a letter from a company advertising cemetery plots and mausoleum space. I'll read it; here goes:

"At the Stiff's Family Cemetery, we'll be the last ones to let you down. In business over 150 years, we adhere to a very rigid policy. If you're scared stiff at the thought of dying, stop by and speak to us. If you're worried your family can't afford stiff prices, stop worrying. During our long history of service to families of the dearly departed, we've yet to stiff anyone!

"We've exciting news! If you wish to take advantage of our special introductory offer of $599.00, you must call within the next hour. In the event the line is dead, call back tomorrow; the phone company is burying cable. Sorry for any inconvenience.

"That's not all! Our new mausoleum is close to completion. It should be ready within ten years. Don't fret if you can't wait, we'll store your remains in Tony the Butcher's freezer located on the dead end street next to our facility.

"Use the enclosed coupon. At no additional cost, we'll throw in a relative. No need to bring measurements; one size fits all. Select your space from Mezzanine (ground level), Bleachers (mid level) or the always-popular Sky Boxes. Choose your neighbor; bring a friend. Don't be a diehard. Dress is optional. Several plans are currently available: No down payment, monthly installments, or if you prefer, use the lay-away plan (after we lay you away, your relatives pay).

"My brothers, Yura and Ima Stiff, will provide perpetual care.

"Now through September, get added value. With each paid burial, the second is half-price (of equal value or less)."

After reading the letter Louie said, "I showed it to Herman, and now we're both confused. What do you think I should do? Do you have any suggestions?"

"Well, since you asked," said Sonny, "have you given any thought to cremation?"

"As a matter of fact, I have," said Louie. "When I mentioned it to Dr. Feelfine, he strongly advised against it."

"For what reason?" asked Sonny.

"He warned, at my age, I should keep away from anything fried," said Louie.

"You know something," said Sonny, "why is it I feel like I've been suckered once again? Good night, Uncle Louie. See you next Wednesday."

Chapter 16
Independence Day

With the approach of July 4th, activity at Dumpsters reached fever pitch. The day was designated as a tribute to the many war heroes living in old-age homes throughout the county.

Preparations were underway for the holiday celebration. During the month, residents and staff joined together creating patriotic floats for the Independence Day parade. Mamie and Sally were co-chair ladies of this year's celebration.

Another committee was charged with making plans for the outdoor barbeque. The big day always ended with a feast prepared by area restaurant chefs, followed by a fireworks display provided by the Tannersville Fire Department.

Other groups were instrumental in planning the Tour de Dumpster's six-minute tricycle race, a grueling test of stamina and endurance involving 20 top bikers. Each participating home in the county entered a contestant. The Shin Tricycle Company was the main sponsor of this year's July 4th tricycle event. Louie was chairman of the race. The man to beat this year was Lance Almost from the Old Butt Home. Everyone was out to see if they could knock the champ out of contention. During yesterday's pre-race drug testing, Antonio Lipshitz from the Last Chance Home was disqualified. Louie told Sonny his tests showed signs of stool softeners. The committee felt this would give Lipshitz an unfair advantage. The softener would enhance the racer's chance to blow the rest of the field away. Louie told Sonny about the incident.

Sonny asked, "What effect might the softeners have other than that?"

Louie said, "You must be kidding Sonny. He'd be first to get there."

Sonny said, "The finish line?"

"No, the crapper!" he said.

Herman Short was Dumpster's entry. The little big man had a problem reaching the pedals, so Phil from maintenance fitted them with extenders.

"By the way, Uncle Louie," said Sonny, "where is Herman? I want to wish him luck."

"He went for a cup of coffee; he said he'd be right back. I think I see him coming now." As Herman walked over to the guys, he reached out to shake Sonny's hand.

"How are you feeling, Herman? Ready for the big race?" asked Sonny.

"Ready as I'll ever be," said Herman.

"What's new?" asked Sonny.

"The doctor says I have *rectal dysfunction* which causes *attention deficit*," said Herman.

"If I read you correctly Herman, I think you mean *erectile dysfunction*," said Sonny.

"Whatever," said Herman, "anyway you look at it, I have trouble coming to attention."

"Have you spoken to Dr. Feelfine?" asked Sonny.

"Yes," said Herman. "He gave me a stiffener."

"You mean like Viagra?" asked Sonny.

"Yes," said Herman, "due to my size, he prescribed half the normal dose."

"I don't get it. What the hell has size got to do with it?" asked Louie.

"Uncle Louie," said Sonny, "I think Herman's referring to his height."

"Oh, I see," said Louie.

"Herman, since you've been on the pill, have you noticed any significant change?" asked Sonny.

"As a matter of fact, I have Sonny." As he turned and winked at Louie, he said, "I don't piss on my shoes anymore."

With that, Louie and Herman looked at each other and simultaneously began laughing to the point of crying.

"Oh I get it," said Sonny. "I'll be darned; when will I learn?"

"Louie, Herman, come boys, the parade's about to start," called Sally.

"We'll be there in a jiff," said Herman. "Let's go, Sonny."

"I'll be there in a minute. Jo is meeting me at the front desk," said Sonny.

Everyone hurried to get a good view. The high school marching band could be heard warming up in the distance. Jubilation was mounting as spectators lined the parade route. Suddenly it began.

Dressed in school colors, the Pocono Mountain members started strutting their stuff, marching in time to the patriotic tune of John Philip Sousa's "Stars and Stripes Forever." Immediately, the crowd of well-wishers let out a roar as they waved American flags. Chills ran up Sonny's spine as he and Jo were bursting with patriotism.

Next in the line of parade was Big Bertha dressed as the Statue of Liberty. The remainder of wheelchair drivers followed; dressed in red, white, and blue costumes. They were trailed by a series of floats, constructed by staff members and residents. The floats depicted American symbols, such as the Washington Monument and Liberty Bell. The artistic talents of their creators astounded everyone.

At the finish, participants and guests received cooling refreshments as they reminisced. Louie and Mamie walked over to where Sonny and Jo were standing. Both were beaming.

"Can you guys believe it? Wasn't that a marvelous parade?" Louie asked.

"It was unbelievable," said Jo.

"I second that," said Sonny.

Looking at his watch, Louie said, "Follow me, the Tour de Dumpsters will be starting in five minutes. I have to fire the starter's pistol. Of course, before the race begins, we have to listen to a speech by that old fart, the mayor."

Sonny and Jo were unable to keep from laughing at Louie's description, especially the "old" part. His Honor is at least 28 years Louie's junior. It seems seniors, no matter what their age, always refer to anyone over 65 as an old geezer. Sonny thought, "It must be human nature."

Shortly after a long-winded speech by the mayor, everyone walked over and began lining the perimeter of the raceway. Before long, cyclists dressed in racing gear mounted their tricycles in preparation for the race.

All eyes focused on Almost, who almost didn't make it after developing a bout of Montezuma's Revenge. As a precaution, he changed his uniform color from *pearl white* to *mustard brown.*

As Herman climbed on a stool to board his tricycle, a loud roar went up by the gang from Dumpsters. In staccato fashion, they shouted, "Herman! Herman! Herman!" Somewhat embarrassed, he smiled and waved to the crowd. Sally ran over, climbed on the stool, and gave Herman a big kiss.

As the contestants mounted their bikes, it was evident a fierce rivalry existed between Almost and Herman. They began eyeballing each other, though difficult, since Herman stood four feet tall, while Almost was almost seven. All the riders were ready.

Louie picked up the microphone and said, "Dignitaries, ladies and gentlemen. Welcome to the Tenth Annual Tour de Dumpsters. Will everyone please rise for our national anthem?"

Silence filled the air as the high school band played "The Star Spangled Banner." At its conclusion, cheers went up once again.

When the cheering ended, Louie said, "Gentlemen, get yourselves ready." After a short pause he said, "When I fire the pistol, that will be the signal to start; one, two..." BANG! The ear-shattering sound sent the cyclists on their way.

As expected, Lance Almost took an early lead. Next in line was Cripple Creek's Rusty Nale. In third place was Last Roundup's Big Jim Schnauzer. Fourth place found Dumpster's Herman Short, Final Stop's Too Tall Johnson was fifth, followed by the remainder of the field.

Ten minutes into the six-minute race, Herman made his move. As his short little legs pumped away, he moved up through the pack until he reached the leader. He was neck-and-neck with Almost, who almost had a stroke when he spotted Herman alongside.

Thirty minutes had passed, with only two minutes to go. Short looked back, then surged ahead and sprinted up the 15 hairpin curves to the finish line, beating Almost by almost 30 seconds. Completing the six-minute race in one hour, Short set a new record for the longest six-minute race in the history of the Tour de Dumpsters.

Fans rushed for the restrooms at the conclusion of the race. Wendy Waters was first to enter, followed by Izadore Closer. Later Izzy was seen being ushered out by Ms. Turnbuckle. By the time he got to the men's room, he lost it.

In the meantime, a crowd of well-wishers gathered in front of the grandstand, awaiting the presentation of the trophy to this year's winner of the Tour de Dumpsters, Herman Short. Almost almost won second place, but was nosed out by Big Jim the Nose Schnauzer. Last year's winner, Lance Almost, crossed the finish line in third place. His uniform showed telltale signs associated with the GI's.

The three men approached the grandstand as the mayor called their names. After a somewhat long introduction, trophies were handed out. Herman was the recipient of first place. He received a tricycle built for two. One couldn't help notice the gleam on Sally's face as it struck home.

"Speech, speech, speech," came the chants from his fans.

In order to reach the microphone, Herman climbed on a chair. He said, "I'm proud to accept this trophy on behalf of all my friends at Dumpsters. It was their confidence that spurred me on, inspiring me to stay the course no matter how difficult it got. I would *never say uncle*."

Once again the fans roared and chanted, "Her-man, Her-man, Her-man."

When the ceremonies ended, the crowd made its way to the rear of Dumpsters, adjacent to the kitchen, to partake of the annual holiday feast. The aroma of barbequed meats permeated the air, whetting everyone's appetites. As the drippings from the succulent meats fell on the hot hickory coals, the flames rose to lick the steaks and chops. In another area, cooks were hard at work shucking clams, mussels, and oysters. The lines converged, filling their plates with mollusks. The remainder of the menu consisted of the usual fare, baked beans, corn on the cob, salads, watermelon, chicken, and desserts. Cold beverages, including birch beer on tap, completed the feast. Laundry employees most assuredly would be working double *duty* come tomorrow.

Off in the corner sat Louie, Mamie, Sonny, Jo, Herman, Sally, and Father Richard. This wonderful man of the cloth was always happiest when eating.

"Tell me Father Richard," said Herman, "what's a rectory?"

"I'm surprised you don't know the rectory is a building where parish priests reside. What do you think the rectory is, Herman?" asked Father.

"A home for unwed fathers," said Herman.

No one said a word; all eyes were on Father Richard. Suddenly he burst out laughing, joined by the rest of the table. Bless Father Richard; aside from his hearty appetite, he has a wonderful sense of humor. Sonny asked Father Richard, "Do you recall several years ago, while delivering the sermon, your microphone malfunctioned? Toward the end of the gospel the sound became erratic, switching volume from loud to soft."

"Do I!" he said. "It was a catastrophe."

"What happened? Tell us Sonny," said Louie.

"It seemed only parishioners seated in the front of the church were clearly able to hear Father. During the gospel desperately trying to adjust the volume, frustrated Father threw up his arms and blurted, '*Something's wrong with this o#?x/@* mic!*' To wit, those in the rear of the church responded, '*And also with you.*'

The table of seven, including Father Richard, broke out laughing hilariously. Once it subsided, Father Richard said, "By the way Herman, I couldn't help notice how much you and Sally complement each other."

"Oh yes Father. Sally and I are like one. I admire her," he said. "She has wonderful attributes. Not only is she a good wife, person, and friend, but she's a real big spender."

As Sally raised her eyebrows, she said, "Exactly what do you mean by that remark, Herman Short?"

"Nothing, my love," he said. "You know how you love to shop. Remember the time you ran up that big bill at the Poverty Barn?"

"Pardon me, Herman," said Jo, a professional shopper herself, "I think you mean pottery."

"No Jo, you heard correctly," said Herman. "The way she spent money, we damn near ended up in *poverty*."

Louie said, "My first wife, Carmela, had one special attribute."

"What was that Louie?" asked Herman.

"Excuse me Father. Carmela was a pain where the sun doesn't shine, if you get the drift."

Everyone chuckled. Several hours passed since the outing began. They were all having a wonderful time.

Father Richard said, "Well folks, I really enjoyed spending time with you. I'm sorry to say I must leave. I must pay my respects to the family of one of the parishioners who recently passed away." After saying farewell, he got up and left.

Sonny said, "Uncle Louie, what happened when I dropped you and Herman off for your overnight camping trip at Big Pocono State Park?"

"Well," said Louie, "once we unloaded our gear, we set up shop, started a fire and pitched our tent. Shortly after you left, we sat around the campfire roasting marshmallows and telling stories. We even made lanyards. Sometime around midnight, we readied ourselves for bed and climbed into our sleeping bags inside the tent. Before doing so, we doused the fire and turned down the flame on the kerosene lamp. Not long after, I heard the sounds of the forest. I said my prayers and fell into a deep slumber."

"Wait a second, Uncle Louie," said Sonny. "What do you mean by sounds of the forest?"

"Herman's snoring," he answered. "Then it happened. Sometime during the night, I heard Herman calling, 'Louie, Louie!' Thinking I was dreaming, I turned on my side.

"Again, only much louder, I heard 'Louie, Louie, are you awake?' 'I am now,' I said rolling onto my back. 'What the heck's the matter? Why did you wake me?' Herman said, as he pointed skyward, 'Louie I was wondering, can you see the North Star?' Half asleep, I said 'You mean to say you purposely woke me to ask if I could see the North Star? I don't believe you Herman!' 'Well can you?' Herman asked. As I looked up I said, 'Yes, I can see the damn star, now go back to sleep.' 'I can't,' said Herman. 'I can't stop thinking.' 'What do you mean you can't stop thinking? What the hell are you thinking about?' 'Well' said Herman, 'nothing I guess, except if you can see the North Star and I can see the North Star while we were sleeping, some son of a bitch stole our tent.' 'For crying out loud Herman,' I said, 'go back to sleep will you? I'm beat.'

"After 20 minutes of continual twisting and turning, I fell off again, when suddenly my fellow camper decided to reawaken me. 'Louie' he said, 'I'm scared shitless!' 'What is it now?' I asked. 'You're becoming a royal pain in the butt. Can't you see I'm trying to get back to sleep?' 'Louie' he said, 'do you hear that?' 'Hear what?' I said. 'That awful screeching sound,' he said. Once again a sound similar to an alley cat in heat rang throughout the campsite. 'You mean that? It's just an owl calling to its mate,' I said. 'An owl?' Herman said. 'Any owl I ever heard went *Whoo Whoo*.' 'You're right Herman,' I said. Then Herman said, 'That doesn't sound like *Whoo Whoo* to me.'

"That did it. By now, I was really pissed. I sat up and said, 'Herman, you little pain in the ass, it's just an owl; a very wise old owl. He damn well knows *who!* He's wants to know *when?* Now go back to sleep, will you?' Angry, I said 'Damn,' as I flopped back down and pulled the blanket over my head in disgust."

Sonny and the girls began laughing. At the end of the fireworks display, Sonny said, "Come, Jo, we'd better get going,"

It had been a truly wonderful day, thanks to the committee's planning. By the looks of the sky and thunder and lightning in the distance, it seemed like they were in for a severe rainstorm.

After kisses and hugs were exchanged, Louie and the others entered the building. Sonny and Jo got into their car. No sooner had they pulled out of the parking lot when the downpour began. It came down in buckets as they drove home. The trip back was somewhat treacherous, but thank goodness, they made it home safely.

Chapter 17
You're Not Going to Believe This

Girl Troops throughout Pennsylvania made preparations for their annual cookie sale. The week before, UPS dropped off cartons of delectable treats at Dumpsters. When Tuesday morning rolled around, everything was ready to go. The evening before, Phil from maintenance hung their banner, placed the American flag nearby, and set up necessary tables and chairs. Early that morning, with help from members of the kitchen staff, the girls arranged the cookies on the tables. Once everything was in place, the troop was open for business. A new recruit, Katie O'Toole, joined Mamie and Sally. As they sat waiting for their first customer to appear, the girls struck up a conversation.

"Katie, were you able to get to the cemetery yesterday to visit your husband's grave?" asked Mamie.

"Yes I did. The darndest thing happened to me. Shortly after I arrived, I…"

"Excuse me," a customer said, interrupting the conversation. "I'd like to buy some cookies. I'm simply crazy about them!"

Her full figure left little doubt.

"I'll take five boxes of Mints and five boxes of Love Knots. I guess that'll hold me till Friday. By the way," she said, "you'll still be selling them, won't you?"

"Yes," said Mamie.

"Goody," she said as she reached into her purse. "How much do I owe you?"

Mamie said, "At $3.00 per box, ten boxes will be $30.00."

Handing Mamie the exact change, she opened her bag and removed a box of Mints. Ripping open the flap, she grabbed a handful of cookies and began munching on them. With her mouth filled, she thanked them as she waddled down the corridor.

Watching in amazement, Sally said, "Do you think we should place another order?" As she disappeared from view, attention again turned to Katie.

"Please continue, Katie," said Mamie. "What were you about to say?"

Caught off guard, Katie said, "Let me see, where was I? Oh yes." Continuing in her Irish brogue, she said, "You know me old bucko has been dead nearly 25 years. 'Til this day, there's hardly a minute goes by I don't think of him. Well now, I'm getting off track," she said as tears filled her eyes. "You've heard of an out-of-body experience, haven't you?" she asked.

"I have," said Mamie.

"Once I left the van, I walked toward Patty's plot. Slowly I made my way over the uneven ground, noting many newly-opened gravesites."

"Business must be booming," said Sally

"As I continued my trek, drawing ever closer, I felt cold all over," Katie said.

"You mean you had chills?" asked Sally.

"Yes", she said. "As the sun played hide-and-seek behind some ominous-looking clouds, I began shaking uncontrollably. I thought, 'My, goodness, what's happening to me?' That's when it hit me."

"Pardon me," a youngster's voice chimed in. "I'd like to buy a box of cookies for my grandma." Surprised, the girls turned to find a young boy standing in front of them, holding several bills in hand. "The cookies are for Grandma Biggs," he said.

Startled, Mamie said, "Certainly, young man. Are you Bertha Biggs' grandson?"

"Yes ma'am," he said.

She handed the youngster the cookies in exchange for his three dollars. Standing in the hallway waiting was his mother. "Thank you," he said as he walked to her side.

Calling over, Katie said, "He's a fine broth of a lad. A real fine young gentleman."

"Thank you," his mother answered as they turned to walk away.

"Please continue," said Sally. "You mentioned you had chills. This is so exciting."

"Have either of you ever had chills?" Katie asked.

"Oh yes," they answered in unison.

"Suddenly I had the urge to pass a bit of water."

"You mean take a pee?" said Sally.

"That's right," said Katie. "Checking the landscape, I noticed the entire cemetery was devoid of visitors. That is, with the exception of the driver who stood patiently leaning against the van. As I hurriedly approached 'himself's' headstone, I took another peek. Still within the driver's view, about ready to bust, I ran behind O'Toole's headstone. Thank goodness he had a big one. As I squatted I dropped my drawers none-too-soon at that, and started in. As anyone caught in the same predicament can attest, the feeling of relief is hard to describe."

"It's nearly as good as sex," said Sally.

"In any case," said Katie, "what a relief. Now picture this: here I am, butt naked, when suddenly a gentle breeze blew. As it did, I felt the sensation of fingers gently brushing against my 'you-know-what.' The few seconds of ecstasy seemed like forever."

Mamie began blushing as Sally said, "Any chance the next time you visit your dear Patty's grave, I might come along?"

Continuing, Katie said, "As the breeze subsided, I pulled a tissue from my purse to dry myself. Rising, I looked down at the spot where I just squatted. Wondering if what I felt might have been a few blades of grass blowing in the wind. To my astonishment there was not a single blade in sight; only a puddle of piddle."

"Wow," said Sally, "this gets better every minute."

"Flabbergasted, I paused to lean against O'Toole's large headstone for support, when suddenly the light went on. I thought to myself, 'Patty, me love, you'll never change your horny ways; you're still up to your old shenanigans.'"

Mamie looked at Sally and then both turned toward Katie.

Laughingly, Sally said, "You Irish are so full of blarney. In fact, Katie, you remind me of Louie and Herman; we don't know when to believe them either."

The three of them laughed so heartily they could be heard clear up the hall.

Strolling down the hall came Louie and Herman.

Arriving at the table, Herman asked, "What seems to be so funny? You keep that up, Sally, and you'll pee your pants."

"I think I already did," said Sally.

"Have you heard the latest scuttlebutt?" asked Louie.

"What's that?" asked Mamie.

"Ms. Turnbuckle told us Art Noodle is returning to Dumpsters."

"You've got to be kidding," said Sally. "I thought he didn't like it here; that's why he went to live with his son-in-law."

"You know what I think?" said Herman. "Artie's a wee bit off his rocker."

"Look, Louie, look who's coming down the hall," said Mamie.

"It's Sonny," said Louie. "Sonny, Sonny, come here!"

Walking over to the group, Sonny said, "Here's nine bucks ladies. Before I leave, I'll take three boxes of Mints. What's new?"

"We were just having a discussion about Artie Noodle. We hear he's coming back for another tour of duty," said Louie.

"What happened?" asked Sonny. "I thought you said he was happy living with his kids."

"According to Ms. Turnbuckle, he was, that is until the state revoked his driver's license."

"How old is Mr. Noodle?" asked Sonny.

"I don't know," said Herman.

"Somewhere in his mid-nineties," said Sally.

"Did Ms. Turnbuckle say why he lost his license, Uncle Louie?" asked Sonny.

"Yes, she said his daughter told her, he was pulled over for reckless driving." "Oh my," said Sonny. "Did he cause an accident?"

"Not exactly," said Herman. "He ran over a tennis racket."

"A tennis racket? That's certainly no reason to revoke a person's license. That's hard to believe," said Sonny.

"I think it's ridiculous," said Herman. "I'll bet it's because of his age. I think there's a conspiracy to get us. I think Art should hire a good Jewish lawyer and fight the case."

"You mean the way you did with the 'WHY'?" asked Louie.

"By the way," asked Sonny, "where did the incident occur?"

"In the park," said Louie.

"Was he given a citation?" asked Sonny.

"Are you kidding? They threw the book at him," said Louie. "He's responsible for all replacement costs."

"Come now, how much could an old tennis racket someone probably threw away cost?" asked Sonny.

"There's more to it than just the cost of the racket. He's being hit with a bunch of hidden costs," said Louie.

"Hidden costs? I don't get it," said Sonny.

"Well," said Louie, "there are additional expenses, such as 20 prize shrubs, an exotic floral display, a chain link fence, posts, and three light poles. Then there's the water fountain, bathroom facilities, including the plumbing that was destroyed, the lawn that was torn up, and the tennis net. The thing that drove the judge crazy is when Artie complained that according to his insurance policy, it wasn't his fault. He told the judge he had no-fault insurance. Artie argued, 'If anyone's to blame, it's the person who left the tennis racket on the court in the first place.'"

"Whoa, hold on a minute," said Sonny. "The whole thing sounds a bit screwy to me."

The two old cronies smiled.

Sonny said, "See you later, folks." He turned and walked away.

"Wait up," said Louie. "I forgot to ask how the kids are doing. I remember you telling me you were going to visit them."

"Fine, Uncle Louie. They mean the world to us. My daughter, Joanne, found a perfect partner. Anthony is a hard-working young man. He has a physical therapy practice in Hackettstown, New Jersey."

"How old are the kids?" asked Louie.

"Erica's eleven and Mark is six. They're smart, polite, and loving grandchildren."

"That's wonderful," said Louie. "Tomorrow Herman and I are playing in a tournament. I'll let you know how we make out when you visit next week. By the way, you sure are lucky. Some guy I know told me the only thing he enjoyed about his kids was making them. Good-bye."

The following Wednesday, when Sonny returned to Dumpsters, Louie explained about the golf tournament Herman and he played in. He said the tournament was sponsored under the auspices of the County's Assisted Living Department. Over 50 golfers participated.

"How many facilities were involved?" asked Sonny.

"Twenty-five," said Herman. "Louie and I represented Dumpsters."

"How did you guys do?" asked Sonny.

"Not bad," said Louie. "Early Monday morning, we were up at the crack of dawn. We're used to hopping out of bed; we spend half the night going to the john. After breakfast, we gathered our gear and waited for the bus to transport us to the course."

"What course did you play at?" asked Sonny.

"Slips my mind. Do you remember the name, Herman?" asked Louie.

"Come now Louie, you expect me to remember? For crying out loud, I can't even remember what day it is," said Herman.

"It's located on Route 611, it'll come to me. Our pee time was 9:30."

"I think you mean tee time," said Sonny.

"No, that was at 10:00," said Louie. "Herman and I hooked up with two old geezers from No Body's Home for the Aged. When we got to the staging area, our carts were waiting. The attendant strapped on our bags. Herman the spendthrift gave him a ten-cent tip.

"Waiting to tee off, I heard some young punk make a wisecrack. As I turned, he gave us the finger. Herman has a low boiling point. He got out of the cart and went over to talk to him. When he got back, I asked if everything was all right. He said, 'Now it is.'"

"What did you tell him, Herman?" Sonny asked.

Herman said, "I told the little punk if he didn't want to find out why your uncle's name ended in a vowel, he'd better knock it off."

"Did he?" asked Sonny.

"You betcha!" said Herman.

"How old was he?" asked Sonny.

"I don't know. What would you say Herman, how old was he?" said Louie.

"Well, if I was to venture a guess, I'd say seven or eight," said Herman. Befuddled, Sonny remained quiet.

"Over the loudspeaker," said Louie, "the starter called our foursome. 'Fettuccine, Short, Cook, and Al Dente.' After the coin toss, Cook and Al Dente led off. Cook got off a beautiful drive, drilling the golfer up front in the head. The ranger then called 911. The ambulance squad arrived immediately and took him away. Al Dente hit a rainmaker, which landed on the roof of the locker room. Next came Herman. Having been born in Scotland, he's played a lot of golf. He got off a nice straight shot right down the middle. Finally my time came. After several practice swings, I addressed the ball, my backswing was slow and direct. My downswing was rapid. I brought my club back slowly, and then came down to meet it, but to my surprise, it rolled off the tee. After placing it back, I went through the same ritual. At last, after numerous Mulligans, pelicans, and a Schwartz, I hit the ball into the water.

"By now, the caravan of players waiting behind us was growing. We finished the first hole and moved on to the second tee. Cook was steaming when his ball dropped into the water. Al Dente hit a long drive, coming a foot from the flag hanging outside the clubhouse entrance. Short hit a long one, but still came up short of the green. My next ball really flew as I struck it on my first swing."

"How close did you come to the hole?" asked Sonny.

"A mile!"

"A mile?" asked Sonny.

"Yes, that's about how much I missed it by. It landed right in the middle."

"Of the fairway?" asked Sonny.

"No, the highway," said Louie. "Herman crawled under the fence and ran onto the highway to retrieve it. Just then a car passed and blew the horn. That same little kid was in the back seat. Again he gave Herman the official one-finger salute.

"When Herman got back, he was filled with 'road rage.' From that hole on, the real Herman showed up. His game was flawless. His enthusiasm rubbed off on us all. The course was a tremendous challenge, even though it was smooth as a carpet. As we came down the home stretch, the spectators' gallery was filled. Off in the near distance, we heard the crowd roar."

"What happened? Did somebody make a good shot?" asked Sonny.

"No," said Louie, "somebody took one. Some guy named Kelsey got hit in the nuts with a club."

"He must have been standing pretty close," said Sonny.

"You might say that," said Louie.

"During final play, Herman got ticked. He flung his wedge up in the air and it landed in the fork of an old oak tree. Unable to reach it, he was forced to use his ball retriever. Of course, that cost him a stroke, though it didn't last long; he was soon over it. Short's short game was superb. On the 18th hole, when his six-foot putt dropped in, he began pumping his fist. As for me, my six-incher ringed the cup to save par."

Sonny asked, "After the final scores were tallied, who was low man?"

"Herman," Louie said, "He set a new course record for seniors, 80 and up."

"What did you shoot, Uncle Louie?" asked Sonny.

"Louie shot a 65," said Herman.

"That's fantastic," said Sonny.

"Hold on Sonny, that was on the front nine. His final score was 134."

While Herman laughed Louie said, "Herman, tell Sonny who gets to play free next time. Ha, ha,"

"That's true. Louie got a hole-in-one on the 19th."

"Nineteenth," said Sonny. "Wait a minute, where did you say the course was located?"

"On Rt. 611, across from the stone quarry," said Herman.

"The only place on 611 across from the quarry is Minnie's Miniature Golf Course!" said Sonny.

"Just a minute, my boy. It may be miniature to you, but when you're 93, it's like playing the Augusta National," said Louie, throwing out his chest and pumping his fist.

"The next time you play there, I'd like to join you. I'll bring my grandchildren along," said Sonny, as off he went to relate the golf story to Jo.

Chapter 18
Not Another Comedian?

By 7:30 Wednesday evening, the auditorium at Dumpsters was overflowing with residents, family, friends, and staff members. Among those in attendance were local dignitaries, TV, radio, and newspaper reporters, all gathered to watch the television debut of Louie Fettuccine and company. That segment of *Jack and the Thin Man* was about to be aired on national TV. As the hour approached, excitement grew.

The administrator walked on stage, acknowledging those in attendance. After doing so, he called for Louie to come forward.

Once Louie joined him, he said, "Mr. Fettuccine, I can't begin to tell you how delighted we at Dumpsters are with your good fortune. Louie, would you be kind enough to describe your feelings, at your first taste of stardom?"

Louie stepped forward and shook hands with the administrator. As he approached the microphone, the applause began.

"Honored dignitaries, guests, fellow residents, relatives, and my wonderful wife Mamie, thank you." Looking at his watch, he said, "In approximately 15 minutes, the moment we've waited for will be upon us— our television debut. Most are already familiar with the facts as to how it came about. For those of you who are not, allow me to explain. In December, on a flight from Newark to Hawaii, we had a three-hour layover in Los Angeles. During that time, Mamie, my nephew Sonny, his wife Jo, and I were asked to appear in a segment of *Jack and the Thin Man*. To explain the entire story would require several hours. Rather than bore you with details, watch and enjoy. It's about to begin. By the way, I'll be available to sign autographs at the show's conclusion. Thank you." As he made his way back to his seat to join the others, he got a rousing applause.

The credits flashed across the screen, followed by the usual three minutes of commercials. The opening segment began. Nervous, Louie rose from his seat, excused himself, and went to the men's room. By the time he returned, the broadcast ended. Everyone, with the exception of family, had departed.

"Where's everybody?" he asked. "Were we that bad?"

"We'll never know," said Sonny. "The scene we were in is probably still lying on the cutting room floor!"

"You must be kidding," said Louie.

"No," said Sonny.

As his jaw dropped, Louie said, "I'm totally embarrassed. How am I going to face anybody again?"

"I'm sure they'll understand, Louie," said Mamie.

"I hope so," he said. "How could they do such a thing?"

Suddenly the auditorium doors swung open as residents made their way back, led by Sally and Herman, singing "For He's a Jolly Good Fellow." While the others took their seats, Herman went up on stage. After lowering the microphone, he said, "Louie, we have to admit you're one hell of an actor. For weeks you had everyone believing you were going to be on TV. We fell for your antics hook, line, and sinker. Anyone who could pull off what you did deserves to be in Hollywood. Let's hear it for Louie, folks, hip, hip, hooray! Hip, hip, hooray!"

"Hip, hip, hooray!" They all chimed in.

"Now my friend, please join me on stage."

Louie made his way to the stage. A single thought came to mind—how in the world was he going to get out of this predicament? On stage, he shook hands with Herman, who handed over the microphone. Thinking to himself, Louie felt the only way to get out of this mess was to tell the truth!

"Whether you believe it or not, everything I've said is the truth. With regard to this evening, rest assured I'm not taking it lying down. I'm fit to be tied; an injustice has been committed," he said. "Monday morning, I'll be on the phone with Actor's Equity to pursue this."

"But Louie," said Herman, "you're not a member."

"It matters not," said Louie. "We donated all our earnings to them. In the meantime, I'd like to thank all of you for understanding."

Herman walked to the center stage microphone and said, "How do you like this guy? He's starting to believe this entire cockamamie story himself!"

As Louie stepped back, the audience didn't know whether to clap or laugh, so they did both.

"Louie," said Herman, "why don't you tell the folks about your stopover in San Francisco on your way home?"

"I don't think they'd care to hear about that," said Louie.

"How about it folks?" asked Herman. "What do you say?"

The audience began their ovation of approval.

Stepping to the microphone once again, Louie began. "After arriving on the mainland, before returning to the east coast, we spent three glorious days in San Francisco. We had rooms at the Sheraton on Fisherman's Wharf. If you've never been there, you don't know what you're missing. The Wharf itself is a seafood lover's paradise. Using the hotel as home base, we made side trips, visiting the Golden Gate Bridge, the redwoods, Alcatraz, and Chinatown."

Pulling an object from his pocket he said, "While visiting Chinatown, I availed myself of this gizmo. Since then, I'm seldom without it." As he held it high, he asked if anyone knew what it was.

Suddenly, the familiar voice of a heckler called out, "What's the big deal Louie? It's just a freakin' candle."

"That's where you're wrong, little man. What I hold before you is not merely a candle. It's a time-tested ancient Chinese alarm clock."

"Looks like a damn candle to me," said the heckler. "Do you really expect us to believe that's an alarm clock?"

"Hold on a minute. Allow me to explain. I'll read the label on the side of the box," said Louie. 'Congratulations on your decision to purchase this time-tested, fail-safe, Chinese alarm clock. Guarantee—If you use this product according to directions, you'll never be late again. This device has been scientifically engineered and rigorously tested. The Long Dong Corporation promises complete satisfaction. Features—Fast, accurate, with memory recall. Automatic shut-off. Easy to read. Warning—Not to be used by individuals suffering from hemorrhoids. Consult your physician. First-time users should check smoke alarm batteries. Fire extinguisher should be close at hand. For emergencies, dial 911. Store in a cool place.'

"Now I'll read the instructions on the candle itself. 'Length - twelve inches. Note the clearly marked numbers 1-12.' The small print says: 'Insert this device up to the marked time of day you wish to be awakened. When in place, ignite the wick and pray! Bunszai! This is a money-back offer. If not fully satisfied, your money will be refunded *when you return the unused portion.*'"

"By the way, you there, the heckler," he said, pointing to Herman. "For guys like you, they offer candles that burn at both ends."

"That's all folks," Louie said, "thanks for hearing me out."

While the crowd applauded, Louie made his way back to his seat. Mamie and the family waited. Mamie stood up and hugged Louie, followed by the others.

When the audience left the room, Sonny turned to Louie and said, "I don't believe this. They really think you were kidding and made up the whole story. That's amazing. It's well past our bedtime; let's call it a night. I'll be in touch tomorrow," said Sonny.

As they walked back to their room, Louie turned to Mamie and said, "I guess I had it coming. I've led them on many a wild-goose chase. Now when I tell the truth, they don't believe me."

"Yes," said Mamie, "that may be true. But no matter, one thing's for sure, they admire, respect, and love you, old boy." Pressing his hand, she added, "Almost as much as I do."

Once in bed, they remained wide awake. Louie said, "You know something, Mamie? This incident has been weighing on my mind. I've reached a conclusion."

"What's that?" asked Mamie.

"The way we were dressed," he said.

"What are you talking about?" she asked.

"I'll bet you a dollar to doughnuts we were cut from the show due to the way we were dressed. After all, it was supposed to take place in Hawaii and we were dressed for the North Pole," he said. "I figure they're saving our scene for another drama."

"For instance?" asked Mamie.

"Oh, I don't know exactly. Maybe a remake of *North to Alaska*," he said as he turned over, flicked the light switch, and wished Mamie sweet dreams.

Early the following morning, after breakfast, the couple decided to walk around the grounds. Not realizing exactly how cool the weather had turned, their stroll came to an abrupt halt. They hurried back to the warmth of the cafeteria.

Pouring each a cup of hot coffee, Mamie said, "If I had known how cold it was out, I would have put on my snuggies."

"I agree," said Louie. "I should have worn my long johns, the ones with the trap door."

"Trap door?" said Mamie. "What in heavens do you need a trap door for?"

"Well," answered Louie, "you never know when you have to unload a bit of cargo."

"Louie," said Mamie, "I'm sorry that when I was a young girl, I never took time to learn how to speak Italian."

"Yes, that is too bad," said Louie. "I think everyone should learn to speak the language of their ancestry."

"It's still early, the show in the recreation room won't start for an hour," said Mamie. "How about teaching me a few basic terms?"

"Sure enough," said Louie. "Now let's see. *Buon giorno (bwon jor-noh)* means any of the following: good morning, good day, good afternoon, and hello. You should use it until early afternoon."

"I see," said Mamie, "how do you say 'Good evening'?"

"*Buona sera (bwoh-nah seh-rah)*," he said. "You'd use that salutation until 3:00 p.m."

"Then," she asked, "how would you say 'Good night' or 'Good-bye' to someone?"

"*Buona notte (bwoh-nah noh-the,)*" he said.

"I hear people on TV say '*Ciao*'," said Mamie.

"So do I," said Louie. "It sounds like 'Chow' and is just another way of saying *Arrivederla (ah-ree-veh-der-lah)*."

"What does it really mean?" asked Mamie.

"It means 'Until next time'," said Louie, "though many times folks will say '*Arrivederci*'; it's not as formal and means to re-see one another. The word is commonly used to say good-bye to friends."

Looking at the cafeteria clock, Louie said, "The show will be starting in 20 minutes. We'd better get going if we expect to get good seats. We'll continue your Italian lesson another time." They got up and left the cafeteria.

"I hope this guy's jokes are better than the banana they had last month," said Louie.

As they entered the recreation room, Herman ran up to the couple.

"Have you heard?" he asked. "The comedian scheduled to perform had an unfortunate accident. I understand he'll be fine, but he's not coming. Of course everyone's disappointed."

"Hey look," said Louie. "Ms. Witty is going up to the microphone."

Picking up the microphone, Ms. Witty said, "By now I'm sure most of you heard the news regarding the comedian who was to appear. He'll be fine and sends his apologies. He said the next time a car runs into him, he'll make sure he's not sitting in his living room. He only has a few minor scrapes, but he's mentally frazzled."

A chorus of whispers filled the air, echoing the audience's disappointment.

Suddenly a voice shouted out, "We want Louie!"

Not long after, everyone joined in. Gesturing for the crowd to calm down, Ms. Witty turned to Louie, saying, "Mr. Fettuccine, how about it? Your public demands your appearance."

Louie was reluctant at first, but after a little prodding from Herman and the rest of the gang, he rose and went up on the stage.

Grabbing the microphone, he said, "Mamie claims our golden years are a bit tarnished." Looking over in her direction he said, "Sorry old girl, I beg to differ with you. Ever since I hit 90, I've begun revisiting my childhood."

Turning to the rest of the audience, he went on, "I remember when I was a kid. I loved to play hide and go seek. Early this morning, Mamie and I played for quite awhile."

All eyes focused on her. Blushing, she smiled. Noticing, Louie said to the audience, "Don't let your mind play tricks on you. It's not what you think. I hid my glasses. Then for the next hour or so, Mamie and I searched high and low. I see lots of smiling faces; I guess you folks play that old game too. I must say though I've added a brand new twist; I swear a lot."

The audience reacted positively.

"While in the bathroom this morning, as I looked in the mirror, I wondered, who the hell's this guy I'm shaving? You guys know what I'm talking about, don't you?" asked Louie. Continuing he said, "After my delivery, Papa, who was a tailor by trade, refused to have me circumcised. Instead he told the doctor to hem it. 'If styles change,' he said, 'I can always let it out.'"

The audience got a kick out of that.

"I watched Sam the cook as he inserted his thermometer into a roast. I asked why? Sam said, 'That's so I can tell when to take my meat out. It helps keep it from shrinking'. I told Mamie the next time she's shopping, pick one up for me!"

On that note, they broke for an intermission, during which Sonny and Herman pulled Louie aside to praise him. Once everyone returned, he began where he left off.

"Now folks, if you'd permit me, I'd like to pay tribute to our parents, those daring immigrants who came to America from far-off shores.

"Like many foreigners, when my parents arrived from Italy, they were poor. In fact, so poor they could only afford to stock their fish tank with anchovies. Easy to care for, they'd lie on the bottom, never having to be fed.

"Not knowing what hardships they'd face, those wonderful immigrants from faraway lands came to America. With hope in the future, they struggled, uncomplaining. They endured World War I, the Great Depression, and World War II in order to make a better life for us. No matter what, they'd 'never say uncle.'"

Because the audience was in full agreement, clapping turned to cheers, as cheers turned to tears.

"Allow me to call to mind my dear mom's philosophy. Remember this one, ladies? '*I think it's going to rain; I feel it in my bones.*'"

While the women giggled, Louie said, "Mom was more accurate than any weatherman. '*Put on clean underwear*', she'd say, '*you never know when you might have an accident.*' Mom, if you're listening, I think I just had one!" Once the laughter died, Louie continued. "'*Don't get your feet wet, you'll catch a cold.*'" Everyone snickered. "Don't laugh," said Louie, "Mom not only knew how to prevent a cold, she knew how to treat one."

"You can say that again," shouted an audience member.

"Mom had a remedy for just about anything. Here's just a few. When I had a bellyache, she gave me Castor oil. My favorite laxatives were those tiny little chocolate bars; you know the ones I mean. I wish they had made some with almonds.

"A stuffy nose meant hanging my head over a pot of steaming water, impregnated with Vicks. Mom covered my head with a Turkish towel. 'Breathe deeply,' she'd say. As I did, I damn near suffocated. When I had a cough, Mom gave me a spoonful of honey and lemon.

"When I was bound by constipation, Mom uttered those familiar words of consolation, 'It's time for a good cleaning out.' Dumpsters takes the stewed prunes approach. Not Mom, her secret weapon was the *soap suds enema.* It was really cool as I watched bubbles coming out from *behind.*"

Everyone smiled.

"To this day," said Louie, "I still wonder why mom used Ivory soap; probably because it floated. How many remember the saying *'You've been overlooked?'"*

All hands raised high.

"In an Italian household, whenever we complained of a headache, Mom would say we had been overlooked. Someone had given us the 'evil eye.' We referred to it as *mal'occhio*. I still recall the first time Mom said, 'I'm going to do the eyes!' I thought, oh boy, Mom's going to do her Eddie Cantor impression. I soon found out differently.

"Out came her voodoo paraphernalia. Included were a soup dish, water, and Italian olive oil, *extra virgin* of course. Taking pains to fill the dish with just enough water, she placed it alongside the chair I sat in. After a few secret words, she'd fill a tablespoon with oil. Next, using her small finger, she'd dip it into the oil. Now came the really scientific part. Carefully, with a gentle flick of her pinky, she dropped the oil in three precise areas of the dish. As I sat quietly, Mom circled the dish overhead.

"The theory was quite ingenious. While Mom mumbled some mumbo-jumbo, the three droplets of oil were to retain their form. If they did, it signified it was nothing more than an everyday headache. If one drop separated during the pass, it meant someone had overlooked me. Two separated drops meant a few people were in on the deal. Three separated drops meant brother beware; you done got the 'evil eye' big time. At times, the spell was so overpowering, it made Mom choke. One time for sure I thought she was gonna croak. On the other hand, if I started yawning, that meant the spell was broken and my headache soon would disappear.

"You know something; I'll be damned if it didn't always work. So remember, when a person you feel is envious of you says, 'Boy, you look good for your age,' beware! Take no chances. Secretly straighten your index and small fingers while tucking the others into your palm and when they're not looking, shove them at them. That means, *right back up yours!*"

Entranced by Louie's enactment, the audience broke up.

"Mom was a wonderful cook. I'm sure just like yours," said Louie. "She never used a cookbook or measured anything. Her cooking came from the heart. Unlike today's complicated recipes, the food she prepared was simple, wholesome, and most of all, *saporito* (tasty)." He gestured by kissing his fingers. "Just a pinch of this, a little of that, a quick taste, and voila, it was a meal fit for a king. Before you could say 'babam,' mom's *pasta fagiole* (macaroni and beans) made you go 'baboom.'"

Once again the audience laughed.

"Though never realizing, Mom was an entrepreneur. When I was a youngster, just as I left the house, Mom would say, 'Come home *early* Luigi, I'm making my *special, chicken* cacciatore.' At the time I never realized, Mom was running an *Early Bird Special.*"

As the message got through, the folks roared.

"When Pop screwed up, Mom would say, 'Emilio, you can't do more than one thing at a time!' Hmm, I see lots of smiling faces out there. I must have hit a chord. Of course, women never have that problem. Or so *they* say. By the way, just who are *they* anyway?"

"From time in memoriam, humankind has pondered that age-old question, just who the hell are *they?* Researching Webster, I discovered *they* are third persons, human beings, any living or extinct member of a household, or a social unit. Yes, ladies and gents, *they* are just plain folks like you and me," said Louie. "That's who *they* are; or so that's what *they* say.

"Bless mom; whenever she whacked me, she'd hit high C, never missing a beat. I don't know about you folks, but in our house, Mom was chief disciplinarian. Mom's weapon of choice was a good old wooden spoon. Her kitchen drawer had a never-ending supply. The ones not broken over my head had notches, like those found on a gunfighter's pistol. At times, while using my head for a drum, she'd issue a news bulletin. '*Wait till your father gets home!*' she'd say. That signaled she was getting tired and needed a relief batter. Today, liberals call it child abuse. Poppycock!

"Now, people," said Louie, "some young folks think old folks are senile, but we're going to prove them wrong. Think for a minute of that special hiding place you ran to whenever you got into trouble. Let's see; was it under the stairs, the hall closet? I'll bet it was on the wooden floor under Mom's bed. Remember how she took the corn broom handle and tried to reach you? Do you recall how you quietly maneuvered from side to side to miss getting poked? Finally, when all was clear, you'd sneak from under, covered with dust balls, but unscathed.

"My special hiding place was in our one bathroom. Once I turned the skeleton key in the lock I was home free. At times, it would get a bit crowded, especially if Mom was after my sister Genevieve and me at the same time. When Mom found the door locked, boy that burnt her up. She started banging on the door, shouting, 'Come out of there, come out this very minute!' Remember, I told you she could do more than one thing at a time. Come to think of it, so could I. While shaking in my boots, I shit my pants!'"

Laughter again filled the room.

"There were times Mom, unable to get us to come out, became frustrated and gave her final ultimatum. It went something like this: 'Wait till you come out, you just wait; you're really going to get *it!*' 'Come out,' I thought, 'I'd be crazy to do that.' Sure, I was young, but not stupid. Besides, the last thing I needed was any of that *it* stuff.

"During the course of our one-sided conversation, Mom felt the need to give another news brief. 'Here comes your father,' she'd shout. 'Emilio, is that you?' she'd call out as the door barely closed.

"No sooner had Pop entered the house, when Mom let it all hang out. In case I failed to mention, Mom was a drama queen. Her impersonation of Tarzan was without equal. Pounding her chest while pulling her hair, she'd scream, 'Emilio he was so bad,' she'd say. 'You can't imagine what he did!' Being of an inquisitive nature, Pop would ask, 'What did he do?' Good old Mom would answer, 'Never mind what he did. What are you going to do?' she'd say. 'What would you like me to do?' Pop would ask.

"Somehow, that was not the answer Mom wanted to hear. At that point, as Mom's focus switched to Pop, she began to vent her anger on him. Though I felt sorry for him, it afforded me a perfect opportunity to make a clean getaway.

"Pop was a great guy, but he had one major fault. He was incapable of making a decision on his own. Let me give you an example. Say I wanted to meet the guys up at the corner. I'd go over to him and say, 'Pop, is it okay if I go out tonight? I'm going to meet the gang and go to the movies.' I guess most of you heard this before—'*Don't ask me, ask your mother,*' Pop would say. Once I learned the game, I played one against the other. I was seldom turned down. You remember don't you? It went something like this, 'Hey Pop is it okay if I go out with the guys tonight? We're going to the movies.' Before he could catch his breath, I'd say, 'Mom said it was okay with her,' then quickly I headed for the door.

"I don't know about you, but each night, till this day, whenever I say my prayers, I thank God for my Mom and Pop and all the folks of that generation. They were the gallant immigrants who by choice, came to

America and helped make this country the greatest nation on the face of the earth. Thank you, my friends, for putting up with my antics."

At the conclusion, Louie was given a resounding applause of appreciation.

Chapter 19
The Last Hurrah

Soon to be 100, Louie began developing serious medical problems, mostly the kind associated with advancing age. Sonny stopped in to see him more frequently. He was hungry to extract every ounce of information from his uncle's failing memory.

During one of their final meetings, Sonny asked Louie to tell him of the time he visited his father's birthplace. Slow to start, Louie said, "Let me explain how it came about. Twenty years ago, I received a letter from Nicolas Feta's son. You recall my telling you about him, don't you Sonny?"

"Yes I do," said Sonny.

"His father and Papa were close friends as well as a number of immigrants from other countries. Nickie Jr. called and explained that plans were underway for all the children to visit the birthplace of our fathers. Once arrangements were completed, we were on our way.

"Our first stop was Ireland, the birthplace of Timothy O'Houligan. Ireland's a beautiful country, covered with green landscapes. From Shannon Airport, a minibus transported us to the village of Blarney. We had reservations to stay at Mary Murphy's Oceanside Bed and Breakfast. Though hard to imagine, there was only one facility to be shared among eight adults. At the time of check-in, we didn't give it a thought. Other than the Murphys' bedroom, there were accommodations for six. We slept two to a room. The room Francois and I occupied was small, but somehow we managed. The spectacular view, overlooking the seascape, overshadowed all else.

"On our first night, Mary's husband Patty invited the six of us to join him at the local pub. Timmy knew it well. Many an evening, his dear departed mother went there to drag the half-crocked Mr. O'Houligan home. After entering the pub, we were introduced to the local gentry. The place was packed; everyone was related to one another. They were a happy-go-lucky bunch.

"Patty Murphy bought the first round of brews. A comely barmaid served our drinks along with a hunk of cheddar cheese and soda crackers."

"That sure sounds wonderful," said Sonny.

"Yes my boy, that it was," said Louie. "During the course of the evening, I noticed a fellow at the bar looking as though he was feeling no pain. He was in the midst of a friendly discussion with a chum. At one point, the conversation became heated. His friend began lecturing him about his being an alcoholic. He insisted he was not. The volume turned up when the friend asked, 'If you're not an alcoholic, then what in the bejeebies are you?' Making an effort to stand erect, answering with thick tongue, he pounded the bar, exclaiming, 'I'm a plain old drunk!' As he lost his footing, his friend grabbed hold, propped him on the stool and asked, 'Tell me then, what the hell's the difference?' About ready to fall flat on his face he said, 'I don't have to go to all those damn meetings!' The whole joint burst out laughing.

"The combination of breathtaking countryside and the hospitality of the villagers helped make our visit a pure joy. On the final night of our stay, we were invited to a church social, where we were treated to an authentic Irish corned beef and cabbage dinner. The meal was delicious. Later that evening, the combination of food and brew had us scurrying to the one bathroom—that is, with one exception, the son of the Frenchman Francois Escargot."

"Was he unaffected?" asked Sonny.

"Yes, that is up 'til 20 minutes before the minibus scheduled to transport us to the airport arrived. That's when the French Revolution began! The young Escargot got that feeling only minutes earlier. I told him I saw Mrs. Murphy enter the bathroom. Not wishing to embarrass one another by knocking on the door, he did the only thing a chivalrous Frenchman could do when caught in such a precarious situation," said Louie.

"What was that?" asked Sonny.

"He shit in a shoebox, inventing the first port-o-john. The stench was so bad when I opened the window, the seagulls took flight. I made a beeline down the stairway. In the meantime the bus arrived. All bags but ours were placed on board. Hurriedly I rushed up the staircase, bumping into Mrs. Murphy, who was gingerly holding a neatly-wrapped package. As I sidestepped, allowing her to pass, I continued to my room. There I found Francois Jr. in a frenzy.

"'*Monsieur* Louie, I'm so, how you say, embarrassed,' he said. '*Madame* Murphy insisted on helping. She took the shoebox with the *poo poo* in it.' 'Quick,' I said, 'Francois, let's get the hell out of here before the *poo poo* hits the fan.' As we rushed down the back stairs with luggage in hand, I told Francois his package was wrapped so nicely, I thought some thoughtful person had given her a gift. Once outside, we boarded the bus. Suddenly, from the corner of my eye, I spotted Mrs. Murphy running toward us holding the beautifully wrapped package. 'Wait! Wait!' she shouted. 'Francois, you forgot your souvenir!'"

"What did Francois say?" asked Sonny.

"Nothing, absolutely nothing. He was petrified," said Louie.

"Nothing?" asked Sonny.

"That's right. As the bus pulled away, I stuck my head out the window and shouted, 'Mrs. Murphy, Francois said it's just a little something in appreciation for your hospitality.'"

Stunned, Sonny looked into the old codger's eyes and politely said, "Uncle Louie, I think you're full of it."

Louie continued, "Our flight left Shannon, for Rome, Italy. Before heading south to Avellino, the birthplace of my Papa, we agreed to visit the capital, with a side trip to the Vatican. After touchdown, we taxied to the gate, disembarked, and were greeted by our tour guide, *Signore Grasso* (fat). He was a short, stocky gentleman whose smile was infectious; though he had one problem. Mr. Fat, as I called him, though very nice, was quite clumsy. He kept tripping over himself. Sonny, if I failed to mention, he was neatly dressed, sported a manicured moustache, and when he smiled, an absence of two teeth was noticeable. But his credentials and knowledge of Italian history were impeccable."

"Did he speak with a broken accent?" asked Sonny.

"Yes; he also made good use of his hands. Mr. Fat showed us to the tour bus where we were introduced to our driver, Valentino. The ladies on the tour were googie-eyed when they met him. Can't say I blame them, he was one very handsome *ragazzo* (boy). After placing our luggage into the underside of the bus, we boarded. As the bus pulled away, Mr. Fat welcomed everyone, wishing us *buono tempo* (a good time).

"We were immediately overwhelmed by the beauty that was Rome. The fountains, the architecture, and the women! *Momma Mia!* (expression for Wow!) Next we entered the old section to view the ancient ruins. The first stop was the Colosseum. Everyone was awestruck; that is with one exception, Hymie Bagelwitz's son Leon. At the base of the structure, literally hundreds of felines pursued thousands of rodents, playing a cat and mouse game.

Leon said, 'They'd never get away with this in New York City, while I was building inspector. I would have condemned this dilapidated building in a heartbeat. *Someone's on the take.*' Realizing he was jesting, we laughed.

"Of course, Sonny, the highlight of our Rome adventure was the tour of the Vatican and our audience with the Holy Father, Pope Secola. Thousands of pilgrims from all corners of the world came to kneel before him and kiss his ring. One by one, as we went forward, carrying on the tradition, something astonishing took place.

"Just as Patel Patel's son Patel Patel, Jr. dropped to his knees, a squealing sound broke the silence. Mortified, Patel Patel, Jr. bowed his head in shame. Suddenly His Holiness pressed his hand to Patel Patel, Jr.'s pate. In a solemn voice said, 'Be not ashamed, my son. It is human to err in the face of greatness. You are not the first nor will you be the last.' As Pope Secola smiled, Patel Patel, Jr. looked up and said, 'Thank you Holy Father. May I ask a favor? When you speak to Buddha, will you tell him it was a slip.' 'Yes, my son, I will, though I think he's already gotten the drift,' said the Holy Father.

"Waiting my turn to receive Pope Secola's *private* blessing, I had an urge to go. Leaving my place in line I headed straight to the men's room. As I stood relieving myself, lo and behold in walks His Holiness. Caught off guard, I pretended not to notice. Lifting his vestments, he stood in the stall next to me."

"I could just imagine your predicament," said Sonny.

"Wouldn't you know, just as he started to go, I sneezed. Startled he spun abruptly in my direction spraying my right leg. Reacting, the Holy Father said, 'Bless you, my son, it's only *Holy Water.*' I thought, 'Now that's what I call a *private* blessing!'

"Our next visit was the Sistine Chapel. Once inside, all heads looked up to view the beautiful fresco, painted by Michelangelo Buonarroti."

Interrupting, Sonny said, "I read that in 1512, Pope Julius II, returning from the Crusades, rushed to view the masterpiece he had commissioned the artist to paint."

"That's right," said Louie, "though according to Mr. Fat, when the pope looked up at the fresco, he summoned the artist to stop immediately. With his work nearing completion, Michelangelo hurried down the scaffolding to speak with the pope. 'Welcome back your holiness. What's on your mind?' he asked. To which Pope Julius said, 'I think-a I change-a-my-mind, stop-a-painting; let's-a-paper instead.' Smiling, Louie took a breath and then continued.

"Boarding the tour bus, we headed across the beautiful countryside in the direction of Venice. Arriving at the dock, we boarded a water taxi that transported us across the bay. After docking, we found ourselves in St. Mark's Square. It was a fun place. Outdoor restaurants ringed the tremendous square. There were almost as many tourists as there were pigeons. The pavement, white from pigeon droppings, was not to be seen."

"What was the main entrée on the restaurant menus?" asked Sonny. "Pasta?"

"No," said Louie. "Squab! While we sat down to partake of a few vittles, the musicians played Italian classics. An individual, kneeling in the square with arms outstretched, was completely covered by a sea of pigeons. After watching Venetian glass being blown by professional glass blowers, we opted to take a ride on a gondola. When visiting Venice, it's a must. As we approached the Bridge of Sighs, I discovered how that ancient structure got its name."

"How did it?" asked Sonny.

"For some unforeseen reason, as we drew near, Ima Kraut's son, a rather tall German, stood up. Smashing his head against the structure, he toppled into the smelly canal. As he did, the rest of us exhaled loudly with a long, deep audible *sigh*, thus discovering how the bridge most likely got its name. The handsome gondolier dove into the water to rescue Ima's son. As he did, I manned the oar, holding the narrow barge steady. We pulled him back onboard, stunned, wet, and smelly. With the exception of a large bump and some scrambling of his brains, he was fine. Patel Patel asked Ima, 'Vy did you stand?' 'I didn't see anything wrong. In Germany, bridges open for tall ships,' he said.

"Leaving Venice, we traveled south to Avellino, the birthplace of my papa. I was so excited. Have you ever been in a *funicular*? It's a small rail car used to climb to the top of a high mountain. It was more exciting and breathtaking than any amusement park ride. Upon reaching the summit, we searched the tiny village of Monte Vergine for remnants of the Fettuccine family."

"How exciting, Uncle Louie!" said Sonny. "Did you discover any interesting information about our ancestors?"

"No, I was very disappointed. However it was so gorgeous there, I felt as if I came very close to heaven that day," said Louie. "Heading down the hillside to catch the returning *funicular*, something interesting caught my eye."

"What was that?" asked Sonny.

"Neighborhood children were playing stickball. A donkey was parked on the street. Alongside, an old geezer was lying down taking a siesta. Several times, the ball rolled near the man. Each time the boy went to fetch it, he awakened the old man asking the time of day. Without changing position, he reached over with his hand, raised the donkey's testicles, giving the boy the exact time. Checking my watch each time, I confirmed the hour. Wondering how was he able to pull it off, I awakened the old man. Using diplomacy while speaking Italian, I asked how was it possible for him to tell the time merely by lifting the donkey's scrotum?"

"What did he say?" asked Sonny.

He said, *"Ascoltare stupido, quando Io alzare guesto l'asimo lepalla, Io vedere quello l'orologio se quello latorre su quello lacollia!"*

"Would you please translate?" said Sonny.

"Certainly my boy! The old geezer said, 'Listen, stupid when I lift the donkey's balls, I'm able to see the clock tower on that hill!'" After a good laugh, though weakened, Louie continued.

"After stops at other countries on the itinerary, we caught our return flight home."

"What a wonderful thing to have done, visiting the birthplace of your ancestors," said Sonny. "Thank you, Uncle Louie. You look tired."

"Yes I am," he said. "Before you go, I'd like you to know something. I'm aware at times I forget what I'm about to say, and I appreciate you giving me a minute or two. Even though I retell a joke or story I've told before, you still laugh or listen. Now that I've become too weak to walk and must lie in bed, you have not forsaken me. For all the times we've shared Sonny, I thank you."

"Uncle Louie, what I've done for you is miniscule when compared with what you have given me."

As Sonny leaned over to hug his uncle, tears fell down the sides of his face. As Louie dropped off into a peaceful sleep, Sonny left the room.

Chapter 20
Even Rainbows End

Nearly seven years had passed since the day Sonny discovered the whereabouts of his uncle Louie. During that first meeting at Dumpsters, a family bond was formed. From that day forward, their two lives became forever intertwined. Sonny was hungry for whatever tidbits of information the elderly gentleman could impart. Louie's vivid descriptions regarding his parents, their dreams, aspirations, and early years in America were things Sonny enjoyed most. Of course, Louie's humorous stories and their escapades also brought Sonny great joy.

Although Louie lived a long fulfilling life, with the onset of each ensuing year, Sonny knew, sooner or later, *even rainbows end*. After all, his beloved uncle was rapidly approaching the century mark. Unbelievable as it seemed, Sonny himself was soon to become an octogenarian. The day-to-day changes in Sonny's stamina were becoming more noticeable. Louie's tremendous zest for living was beginning to wane. Not suggesting either was ready to throw in the towel, for neither would "say uncle." But as most seniors know too well, *old man time is so darn mean*.

During the past several months, Sonny's visits to Dumpsters were becoming more frequent.

While speaking with Jo, Sonny said, "I've begun to notice, little by little, Uncle Louie's conversations are becoming more and more redundant."

"Can you be more specific?" asked Jo.

"Well, for example," Sonny said, "he constantly asks for Mamie, forgetting she passed away."

"What do you tell him?" asked Jo.

"Because I don't wish to upset him, I tell him she's visiting her sister. Once I made the mistake of telling him she died. It was extremely traumatic. I decided in the future, I'd fib a little."

"It's getting worse, isn't it, Sonny?" asked Jo.

"I'll say. He asks, 'Why hasn't my mother been to see me? Where is she?' I tell him she's too ill to visit, which I found suffices."

"What is it? What does Dr. Feelfine say is wrong?" asked Jo.

"He said it's Alzheimer's," said Sonny. "I tell you, Jo, it's hard to watch someone as vibrant and full of hell as Uncle Louie deteriorate like that. Although there are instances when he's perfectly normal. It's during those periods of normalcy, I try to inject a bit of humor, as he had done on so many occasions. Through experience, I discovered it's less upsetting if I go along with him and play the game, even if it means stretching the truth a bit. One thing's for sure, unlike most of us, I've yet to hear Uncle Louie complain.

"When I think back, shortly after finding him, I recall him saying, 'You know Sonny, I don't believe I'll be around much longer.' I asked, 'Why do you think that, Uncle Louie? Do you plan on dying soon?' Immediately he'd say, 'What makes you think I'm going to die?' He'd wink and smile at me.

"There was the time he rejoiced at having received an invitation to take a trip. 'Sonny,' he said, 'have I ever mentioned the letter I received from the son of my papa's dear friend, Nicholas Feta?' Of course he had on several occasions, but I would never let on. He'd say, 'Remember our discussion regarding The Night School for Immigrants?' 'Yes, I do,' I said. 'The offspring are making plans for a trip to the birthplace of our fathers. Here's a copy of the itinerary. Take a look,' he said. 'Do you think you'll be going?' I asked. 'Think! Are you kidding? Of course I'm going. Nothing on earth could stop me. I wouldn't miss that trip for the world,' he said.

"Those remarks still resonate in my ear. Then there was the time I told Uncle Louie I had an appointment with my son-in law Anthony concerning an ongoing discomfort in my butt. To which he said, 'Sorry to hear that Sonny, I know exactly what that's like. I lived with a pain in the ass for years.' I asked, 'Was it sciatica?' 'No,' he said, 'Carmela!'

"Whenever we spoke about immigrants, as long as they entered the country legally, Uncle Louie championed their cause. 'My parents,' he said, 'like many foreigners were immigrants. It was the immigrants whose toil, sweat, and tears built the infrastructure of our great nation. They and those who follow are what make America great.' As his face turned red, tears filled his eyes. Then he said, 'My dear mother, may she rest in peace, told me she wasn't born in America, but made damn sure I was.'

Just then, the phone rang. As Jo went to answer, Sonny continued with his thoughts, realizing it would not be long before his uncle passed away. With that in mind Sonny drifted off thinking of what his uncle had told him about his ancestors' difficulties. He recalled Louie's discussions regarding his family's struggles and disappointments. Sonny got a complete education regarding discrimination practices concerning not only his family, but also every immigrant, no matter where they came from.

Sonny remembered Louie saying, "No matter what, I'll bet all the tea in China there isn't a single person in the lot that has any regrets; and wouldn't do it over again. Here's something to think about, Sonny. You and I and millions like us are citizens because of our birthright, whereas immigrants are citizens by choice. It takes all of us to keep America strong and free. I still recall sitting on Papa's knee as he described my proud heritage. As I explained, Papa was born in Avelino, Italy. His parents, Emilio and Generosa Fettuccine, were hardworking folks who instilled in him a sense of right from wrong. Mama taught us to keep spirits high, have faith in God, live life to the fullest, and find our calling." Sonny thought, "That's the exact same philosophy my dear mother passed on to all my family."

Sonny recalled his uncle saying that while attending school in Avelino, his papa was a good student. After graduating, he was accepted to the renowned School of Internationals in Rome. It was there he struck up a lasting relationship with a fellow student from Greece, Nicholas Feta.

Louie explained to Sonny that on one hot steamy afternoon, as they sat under a tree, hiding from the sun's scorching rays, Papa asked Nicholas if he'd like to go to America. Nicholas agreed and thought it was a wonderful idea. He too wanted a chance to go to the land of opportunity. Louie further elaborated both boys were members of families associated with the food business. The Feta family raised goats. From the milk, they made delectable morsels, which we know today as feta cheese. The Fettuccine family ran a pasta business. They cut the pasta into small ribbons, calling their creation fettuccine. It was sheer coincidence that both last names began with the letters *Fet*, which is synonymous with food.

Louie told Sonny that after their discussion, both young men rose from their resting place and went back to the classroom. That evening, they sat in their room writing letters to their parents, wondering if there might be any resistance to their plans. The next morning, they mailed their letters and then patiently waited for their responses. Not long thereafter, they received their answers. While opening each other's mail, the anxiety grew. After reading the correspondence, they looked at one another. Then suddenly, they jumped for joy at the positive responses they received. Included in their envelopes, Louie said, there was enough cash to book passage aboard the first ship leaving for America.

It so happened, at the conclusion of the current semester, the *Titanic* was embarking on its maiden voyage. Arrangements were made to travel onboard a tramp steamer from the Port of Naples to England. At that point, they would sail to America aboard the great ship. Louie further said they were only able to afford steerage class. Before departing, he said they returned home to bid farewell to their loved ones.

Astonished at the reality of it all, Sonny couldn't believe what he had learned, especially the part about how after the *Titanic* capsized, the two of them were able to hang onto pieces of the ship's debris until help came along. After being rescued, they were placed in sickbay, due to hypothermia. Strange as it seems, they were plucked from the freezing waters by the same tramp steamer that brought them to England, the *S.S. Fetch.* Louie told Sonny that after looking in the dictionary, he found that the definition of *fetch* means *ghost.* Not only was it a ghost ship, but like their last names, it too began with the letters *Fet.*

Louie mentioned that after they landed at Ellis Island, waiting to be processed, they went through the extensive bureaucratic formalities that all new immigrants were subjected to. Sonny thought for a moment, "Unlike today where aliens are able to enter United States at will."

Sonny also learned that once given the necessary papers, immigrants were ferried across the Hudson to the Port of New York. From that starting point, they set out in opposite directions. Friends or relatives who had preceded them to America usually greeted the immigrants. Once greeted by friends, they were taken to their respective homes to start their new lives.

Rehashing the story in his mind, Sonny recalled that Louie explained about the time when his papa was a very young boy, working as a tailor's apprentice in the village tailor shop. Although young, he quickly learned the trade, which he found rewarding. Because of his experience, he found work in a tailor shop in Orange, New Jersey. At the same time, citizenship was always in the back of his mind. When he discovered he could attend The Night School for Immigrants, he wasted no time in applying. As fate would have it, once again the boys' paths crossed. Louie explained the school was a mix of immigrants from various countries, and that his father's classmates, other than Nicholas, included Ima Kraut, Timothy O'Houligan, Hymie Bagelvitz, Francois Escargot, and Patel Patel.

Just then, Jo returned, interrupting his thoughts. "I'm sorry Sonny, it was just Dorothy. She just blew into town and wanted to catch up with the latest happenings."

"That's all right. I was thinking about a few other things that Uncle Louie had told me about."

"Well, what were you thinking about?"

"I was thinking about when his papa came over to America and the things he encountered. For instance, when his papa went to The Night School for Immigrants, where he learned the usual; writing, reading, math, and history. One incident he told me about was that one day the teacher, Ms. Darling called on Patel Patel to describe events leading to the end of British rule in India.

"She wanted to demonstrate the lengths freedom-loving individuals would go to achieve liberty. She asked Patel Patel, 'Would you mind telling the class what happened during the meeting of Mahatma Gandhi's followers in 1947?'

"Patel Patel stood before the class and told them that during a gathering at the Queen Victoria Hotel in Calcutta, the Mahatma instructed his followers, that vhen you check out of the hotel, don't do like the British and steal the towels. Gandhi said, 'Ve need the sheets!' Patel Patel broke the ice and everyone laughed. More than that, they became lifelong friends."

"That's a great story. Patel Patel had quite a sense of humor, didn't he?" said Jo.

"Yes," Sonny said, "and from then on everyone relaxed and put their noses to the grindstone. After several months of hard work, they were ready to reap their reward: U.S. citizenship. The stage was set. Louie's papa told him the ceremonies began with the Pledge of Allegiance and concluded with the singing of Irving Berlin's "God Bless America."

A chill gripped Jo, as it does most people at the mention of that patriotic tune. After their discussion, the two decided to turn in for the night.

With the passing of each day, the changes became more noticeable. Sonny reached a point that when the phone rang, he expected to hear bad news.

It was early Sunday morning when that much-anticipated call arrived. He sat up in bed, reached for the receiver, and heard that all-too-familiar voice of Ms. Turnbuckle.

"Sorry to wake you, Sonny. I hate to be the bearer of bad news. Your uncle's condition took a turn for the worse," she said.

Without asking further details, Sonny responded, "I'll be right over."

Hurriedly, he dressed and drove straight to Dumpsters to find Ms. Turnbuckle waiting at the front door to greet him. As they proceeded to Louie's room, she apprised Sonny of his uncle's failing condition.

"We have him on a respirator," she said. "His temperature's elevated due to the onset of viral pneumonia. Dr. Feelfine has ordered antibiotics, plus something to make him rest comfortably. We've contacted the ambulance company and made necessary arrangements to transport him to Pocono Medical Center."

They reached his room and went in to find him resting quietly. Sonny sat down in a chair close to his bed, noting his breathing apparatus. He was mesmerized by the constant whirring which put him in a trance.

He began reflecting back to happier times, remembering the joy he'd found since that first meeting at Dumpsters. The vivid pictures flashing before his tear-filled eyes were endless. The tears were a mix of sorrow and gratification.

Sonny recalled the fishing expedition, Louie's retelling of his nightmares, the "honeymoan," life with Carmela, the golf stories, plus so many more.

"Sonny, Sonny," was the call, which he could faintly hear, but because he was engrossed in thought, he was unable to assimilate. Suddenly, he felt a gentle nudge at his shoulder, breaking him from his stupor.

"Yes, what? What is it?" he asked. Realizing where he was, he said, "Oh, excuse me. My thoughts were elsewhere."

"It's your uncle. He's coming around," said Ms. Turnbuckle.

As Sonny grasped his hand, Louie smiled, acknowledging recognition of his nephew. Sonny leaned over and whispered in his ear, "I love you, Uncle Louie. Thank you for being so wonderful to me and to all whose paths you've crossed."

Then Louie smiled again and winked at Sonny, before his eyes fell into a fixed position.

With that, Ms. Turnbuckle asked an aide stationed outside the door to summon Dr. Feelfine. He arrived within minutes, checking to make sure the end had come.

As he closed Louie's eyelids, he turned to offer his condolences, saying, "Your uncle's on God's team now." Then he departed.

Ms. Turnbuckle put her arm over Sonny's shoulder, offering her heartfelt sympathy. Sonny walked over to the window, cocking his head up to look at the sky.

"I have a letter your uncle gave me last year. He asked me to give it to you when the time came."

As she reached out to hand it to Sonny, he said, "Would you mind reading it? He thought a great deal of you; I'm sure he'd want it that way."

"Not at all," she said, "I'd be glad to." Using a letter opener to expose the contents, she removed the paper. Unfolding it, she said, "It looks to be a poem." Then she began reading.

"Sonny my boy, I've loved you as if you were a son. This poem is for you.

The boss dropped by to claim my soul,
The deck was stacked, 'twas time to fold.
I played my hand without regrets,
I followed suit and hedged my bets.
Remember life is but a game,
When your time's up, he calls your name.
See you around, kid. — Uncle Louie.'"

Holding back pent-up emotions, Sonny looked back at the sky and then asked Ms. Turnbuckle to please hit the light switch. She complied. Now with the room in complete darkness, Sonny had a clear view of the heavens. As a cloud passed in front of the moon, it faded from sight. Suddenly a shooting star passed to brighten up the night. In its race across the pitch-black sky it slowed as if to wink.

"Come quick," Sonny called, "look, Ms. Turnbuckle!"

Joining him at the window, she too noted this phenomenon. The star's progression slowed. Once again the star seemed to wink. Only this time, Sonny winked back. Before racing off, it reciprocated one last time. Then something startling occurred. The full moon slithered from behind the cloud cover, casting its bright rays on the now smiling face of Sonny's dear uncle. The sheer excitement of the moment was like adrenaline for Sonny's heart. His being was filled with a warmth he'd seldom known, one which you might equate to seeing a loved one for the first time, after being apart.

Now able to factor in the series of events and their significance, the burden of despair was lifted from his wounded heart. The only sensation left was one of happiness and closure.

Suddenly realization set in. Although he'd *never say uncle again,* his heritage would never die. It will live forever through his children and theirs. So be it.

"Epilogue"

Many moons have passed since those good old days. Old neighborhood kids can only sit, reminisce and wonder, *"Where did it go?"*

Seniors face still other challenges. The events of September 11th have changed the world forever. Future generations are worried and rightly so. It is up to the seniors of today to set an example, as those before have done. They must encourage their children and grandchildren to be alert and hang tough. Impress upon them adversity under many guises will rear its ugly head. When it does, and it will, tell them not to falter but instead, *never say uncle*.

Now might be as good a time as any to give the kids a great big hug, tell them you love them, and make them laugh. It's still the best medicine for whatever ails you.

About the Author

Emilio Paletta currently resides with his family in the Pocono Mountains of Pennsylvania. He retired there after spending over 40 years employed in the radiology departments of hospitals and nursing homes. His final endeavor in the medical field came in 1986, when he founded Redi-Tech, Inc., an x-ray technology placement agency employing over 350 technologists, operating within the tri-state area.

Since 1970, Paletta has been a member of the American Society of Composers, Authors, and Performers. He is a member of A.A.R.T. and the Knights of Columbus.

Early in his showbiz pursuits, he wrote, directed, and performed in musical variety and comedy shows. Recently, he performed in productions sponsored by the Pocono Lively Arts Community Theater.

Printed in the United States
20261LVS00003B/217-225